TRENDS & ISSUES

IN SECONDARY ENGLISH

TRENDS AND ISSUES IN ENGLISH LANGUAGE ARTS
1999 EDITION

NATIONAL COUNCIL OF TEACHERS OF ENGLISH
1111 W. KENYON ROAD, URBANA, ILLINOIS 61801-1096

Staff Editor: Kurt Austin
Interior Design: Tom Kovacs for TGK Design; Carlton Bruett
Cover Design: Carlton Bruett

NCTE Stock Number: 55030-3050

TRENDS AND ISSUES IN ENGLISH LANGUAGE ARTS

Keeping track of the myriad issues in education can be a daunting task for those educators already stretched to get thirty hours into a twenty-four hour day. In an effort to inform and support English educators, the National Council of Teachers of English annually offers this volume featuring current trends and issues deemed vital to the professional conversation by our membership at large. Whether specialists or generalists, teachers know that no single "trend" or "issue" could touch the interest and concerns of all members of NCTE; with these books—one for each section of the Council: Elementary, Secondary, College—we aim to chronicle developments in the teaching and learning of English language arts.

The wealth of NCTE publications from which to draw the materials for *Trends and Issues* proves a double-edged sword. Publishing thirteen journals (bimonthly and quarterly) and twenty to twenty-five books annually provides ample content, yet what to include and what not? Of course, timeliness and pertinence to the issues of the day help shape the book, and, more important, we aim to meet our primary goal: Is this valuable to our members? This edition of *Trends and Issues*, we believe, offers readers a seat at the table, a chance to join the discussion. At the college level the trends and issues cited for this year are "Diverse Students, Diverse Teachers," "Ethics in Teaching, Research, and Publishing," and "Service Learning and Social Change." At the K–12 levels members cited "Multimedia in the Classroom," "Second Language Learners," and "How Politics Have Shaped Our Thinking and Our Classrooms" as those topics of current relevance to them as English language arts professionals.

We hope that you'll find this collection a valuable resource to be returned to often, one that facilitates professional development and reminds us that we all have a stake in the language arts profession.

NCTE invites you to send us those trends and issues in the English language arts that you feel are the most relevant to your teaching. Send your comments to our Web site at www.ncte.org (click on "Trends and Issues") or e-mail directly to John Kelley at jkelley@ncte.org.

Faith Schullstrom
Executive Director

CONTENTS

I Multimedia
in the Classroom

The degree to which electronic media presents itself to our students in and outside of school is rapidly increasing. As the increase becomes evident, a tangled bundle of issues emerges: access, integration, teacher and student training, and basic skill development and maintenance, to name a few.

The authors in this section provide some guidelines and suggestions for addressing specific concerns related to larger issues. Each describes current literacy demands that are far more complex than those that previous generations of students and teachers had to address. And while describing the critical thinking and technical processes students must master, the authors all note increased fluency in traditional reading, writing, speaking, and thinking developed through increased pedagogic and curricular attention to media literacy. This is most clear in the selections from Meta Carstarphen and Barbra Morris. As Carstarphen states, "thoughtful interaction with the media can offer pathways to strengthen students' basic capabilities in reading, writing, and reflective observation."

Selections by Nancy Traubitz and Kay Beth Avery et al. also explore ways in which media and technology literacy help develop traditional literacy, but they place special emphasis on access. While Traubitz's article describes a teacher research project that asks "What strategies will broaden the application of technology to a wider group of students?", Avery et al. provide a rich store of activities that integrate media into the traditional English language arts classroom.

1 Media "Target Assignments" Invite Students to Tune In, Turn On, and Write

Meta G. Carstarphen

Much to the chagrin of every classroom teacher, students today seem more intrigued by popular entertainment than by academic assignments. Statistics about the pervasive influences of the media on contemporary youth and adults are not reassuring. As Art Silverblatt reports in his book, *Media Literacy: Keys to Interpreting Media Messages* (1995), "in the average American household, the television set is on for over seven hours per day. . . . And remember, television represents only one media system."

Concern about media influences on our society is not likely to abate, as new technologies force rapid convergence of established communication tools with innovative ones. Industry insiders speak confidently of the not-too-distant future when the majority of American households will boast access to hundreds of new television channels, scores of newspapers via computer, and magazines on demand thanks to our long-distance communication services.

Conceptually, media literacy encompasses strategies to "decode" messages in a meaningful way. A basic definition of such competency, offered by the 1992 National Leadership Conference on Media Literacy, sets forth these parameters: "It [media literacy] is the ability of a citizen to access, analyze, and produce information for specific outcomes" (cited in Vivian 1991, 300). Though intentionally broad, this statement invites a proactive approach from educators who want to challenge their students to attain

Reprinted from Chapter 16 of *Reflective Activities: Helping Students Connect with Texts*, edited by Louann Reid and Jeffrey N. Golub.

mastery over media messages instead of accepting the defeat of their minds by the trivia of mass entertainment. However, it is just as important to recognize that thoughtful interaction with the media can offer pathways to strengthen students' basic capabilities in reading, writing, and reflective observation.

This certainly has been my experience in teaching media survey courses. Typically, such a course is a beginning college student's introduction to the history and operations of each major component of mass communication: newspapers, magazines, radio, film, television, motion pictures, sound recordings, and books. Heavily imbued with historical facts, dates, and profiles, the texts for these courses naturally emphasize (in terms of teaching) presentational styles which are long on lecture and (in terms of learning) individual performance on standardized tests. Add this aspect to the fact that such courses are institutionally arranged to encompass large enrollments, and the opportunities for innovative student participation are usually very limited indeed.

Underlying all of these logistical aspects is a question that, to me, points up a very important philosophical dilemma: how can such a course prepare potential communication professionals for their chosen fields if their thoughts are restricted to marks on a machine-scored test page? How can we groom professional writers and critical thinkers if we don't nurture as much respect for the content of their thoughts as we do for the accuracy of their form?

My solution has been to institute a semester-long research project called Target Assignments. At the beginning of the term, students receive a list of at least fifteen topics related to various aspects of the media. I invite students to reflect upon their reaction to a particular topic. Students get to select ten topics from the list as a minimum but are invited to do more for extra credit if they so choose. Their goal is to have their Target Assignments completed by the announced date, typed according to specifications, and submitted as a total report. Collectively, the Target Assignments are worth one hundred points, or the weight of a unit exam.

What kinds of topics are included? Varied, in both complexity and perspective. Some invite the students to monitor familiar media in an unfamiliar way, such as recording their experiences in listening to five AM and five FM radio stations they have never paid attention to before. Another type of assignment asks them to gauge media effectiveness by analyzing a newspaper article's use of graphics, photos, and charts in order to determine how much these added to their understanding of the story.

Still other kinds of assignments invite students to be social media critics by evaluating the interrelatedness between media and society as they see it. These slightly more rigorous topics challenge students to cite examples of television shows which they feel perpetuate a kind of stereotyping, or evaluate strategies that talk-show hosts may be using to influence their audiences, whether through logical or emotional appeals.

None of the media experiences that the students are asked to write about are inherently new. Our students are professional media consumers. But what is new for them is the occasion to isolate that singular media moment as if it were significant (which, of course, it is) and render an opinion. Their responses show that they can relish such self-reflective moments.

One student, Allison, is pretty insightful about an episode on the Geraldo Rivera show where radio talk-show host Howard Stern was, for a change, the visitor: "As a guest . . . Howard taunts Geraldo. Stern made jokes of the Geraldo 'broken nose' incident and sex life on the host's show. Breaking every rule of courtesy, Stern is changing the behavior on TV. . . . Why people worship Stem is not the issue. The issue is that Stern is changing the unspoken respect that governed media behavior."

David, in another assignment, looks at newspapers' use of graphics and makes some judgments which go beyond what the textbook had to say about the differences among media:

> In the world of slick magazines and slick television, the daily news media is at a disadvantage. Newsprint lacks the immediacy of tele-vision and the sexiness of magazines. However, by effective use of visuals, newspapers are making up some of that ground. The tangi-bility of a map or a chart in front of you is not something that tele-vision can duplicate, and the timeliness of the photos is something that monthly magazines can't do as quickly. By adapting to the graphics needs of a society raised on TV, [the] newspaper is far from being left in the dust.

I am refreshingly surprised by the amount of passion students bring to this assignment as well as the unique insights. One student, Robert, reviewed a documentary called *Ethnic Notions* about the history of African Americans in film and television, making some insightful comments in light of that tradition about current television fare starring African Americans. A female student, responding to the question about identifying stereotypes on television, picked the popular show about teenagers, *Beverly Hills, 90210*. From her perspective, she quite eloquently showed how this program "unfairly" portrayed high school students as privileged, overly concerned about sex, and good-looking.

I grade these assignments to reinforce the basic goals of writing fluency and critical thinking. Therefore, students receive full points for successfully writing coherent narratives to the minimum required length of one-and-one-half pages for each assignment. No opinion is wrong as long as the student cites examples and shows some reflective thought about the topic. At the same time, in classes where enrollment is seventy-five students or more, grades on content and format take precedence over penalties for errors in mechanics and style.

More often than not, however, students willingly exceed my expectations and their own. If I simply announced to the class that each student would be responsible for a fifteen-page research assignment, many would faint in disbelief. Yet they end up writing at least this much, often more, in their cumulative reports. I also ask them to bind their reports attractively, yet I give no specific parameters. Many use their own savvy to create eye-catching covers, attractive margins, graphics, and other elements to influence the appearance of their own media products.

Not every student will produce a television show, write for a newspaper or magazine, or take to the airwaves as a disc jockey. But every student is immersed in media and should be media-literate. Through Target Assignments, students can also use their media savvy to push up their competencies in reading, writing, and critical thinking.

Note

The author gratefully acknowledges the contributions of students Robert Green, David Holt, and Alison Jay, who were enrolled in JOUR 1210.

References

Silverblatt, Art. 1995. *Media Literacy: Keys To Interpreting Media Messages.* Westport: Praeger.
Vivian, John. 1991. *The Media of Mass Communication.* Boston: Allyn and Bacon.

2 Toward Creating a TV Research Community in Your Classroom

Barbra S. Morris

Despite the often-repeated generalization that television viewers are passive, in reality, television watchers already are quite active and vocal with each other in discussing what they see and hear via this medium. It is not uncommon for viewers to talk back to their TV screens while broadcasts are in progress, even though they won't get answers. Consider sports enthusiasts, for instance, who watch sportscasts for hours, shouting at the screen and happily sharing analysis with everyone nearby. The pleasure and energy television viewers bring to talking about television signals an existing motivational avenue into inquiry, a likelihood for a community of classroom television critics in dialogue, who might become non-print text researchers and, even, cultural studies' analysts.

How can this possibility be realized? I offer three instructional stages: 1) establish students as experts; 2) provide a solid research procedure; 3) require written reports and, then, oral presentations of research findings to the class.

Establish Students as Experts

I begin by distributing a questionnaire that students fill out individually before launching into their first group television discussion. My questionnaire draws out individual responses regarding each person's preferences in programming and brings to light a broad range of assumptions about what is good or not so good about the medium. In class, I ask all

Reprinted from *English Journal*, January 1998.

students to respond aloud to the first five questions, and ask for volunteers to answer the rest (see Figure 1).

Typically, as students talk, I write on the blackboard an initial sample of responses to the final question because I want to collect immediate speculations about effects of the medium upon their perceptions and their lives before they start their separate research projects and report upon their insights to the class. Later, following their first oral research reports, I ask them to add to this original list, drawing upon their new experiences.

As I listen to students' talk about various genres of programming that they enjoy watching, or perhaps never watch, I point out that there are many, many program types, each one with its own conventions, image environments, forms of rhetoric, and audiences. Moreover, because some people watch talk shows or sitcoms or news or Comedy Central or sports, and others do not, we will avoid generalizing about effects of television text as a whole on the complete television audience. We envision viewers as clusters of special interest groups who follow certain kinds of programming. For some genres of text, the groups, or shares of the total audience, are larger or smaller; they sometimes may be differentiated in character by age or gender or economic situation, and so on. Perhaps the only televised content that everyone sees, like it or not, is commercials, since they interrupt or "bookend" almost every fifteen to twenty minutes of most network broadcasting.

However, even if people happen to see the same programming, they are unlikely to agree about what was important or meaningful about it. For instance, two students in class looking at a news clip that I tape and screen for analysis may display two very different ideas about it. I show a news story depicting violence and ask what do the images provided to us in the news report lead us to think about the event: one student says that the image of the body of a criminal shot and left by the roadside is evidence that crime does not pay, while another says: "Television de-sensitizes us to this person's death. There is a guy face down in a ditch, and people aren't expected to think how his family must feel at all."

Differences in students' observations, their dissimilar readings of any text, are authentic and impelled trajectories into deeper discussions of how we read texts (Morris 1995). Students share reactions; we are all being led to wonder about why we think as we do about what we see, and for what reasons we make meaning differently. In a sense, critical viewing of

Individual Television Watching History and Opinion Survey

1. What is your earliest memory of a television program you watched?

2. As best you can, describe what you thought about that program at the time.

3. What do you think about that program now? Do you think it should be on television?

4. What do you choose to watch on television when you have time and access to a set?

5. What programs do you *never* watch?

6. Whom do you like to watch your favorite programs with? What sorts of talk might go on during those watching events when you are with others?

7. Who would you consider influential people regularly seen on TV? In what ways do you believe these people influence viewers such as you and others?

8. What imagery comes to mind when you think of the "best" and "worst" of TV? Why do you think so?

9. In what ways do you think television influences society? Think of both negative and positive impacts.

10. What is meant by creating an "image" of someone on television? Use a concrete example of someone you think has an image and explain the dimensions of it.

11. What sort of programming would you like to see on television? What would it consist of?

12. What myths about television exist and why? Name a few you think don't hold water but persist, and explain why you think they do.

13. As a member of the "television generation," what do you think that phrase means? What are the characteristics that phrase implies and are they accurate?

Figure 1. Individual Television Watching History and Opinion Survey

television in the classroom means developing everyone's curiosity about the text and about reasons behind bringing dissimilar perspectives to it.

Research Projects

I want each student to undertake a separate television research project that originates from a text he or she watches regularly. Close analysis is the backbone of television content research; it encourages students to explore the broader arena of cultural studies, examining cultural narratives and assumptions for their influences upon us. Students must do their own research. Unfortunately, schools often mystify research, only asking students to attempt it when they are in advanced classes. However, television content research simply asks students to develop a well-formed question, collect evidence, and interpret findings. The analytic process is neither mysterious nor frightening. Students study closely what is on the screen in order to think together about what is there, what it means, and to generate further intriguing questions.

The content research model I require my students to follow resembles scientific inquiry (Morris 1993). Asking all students to follow a similar process of close questioning and analysis establishes our work as a research community and creates common ground rules for collective intellectual inquiries. Students take on small, manageable research projects, tackling questions that they can reasonably deal with in one or two sittings in front of a TV screen. Since they are analyzing texts they already know well, they do not need basic explanations of content, as they might with unfamiliar print literature. The initial research they undertake is quantitative, somewhat similar to stylistic or linguistic analysis. Their research involves counting appearances of particular features of text and, with that data, exploring how that aspect of television text, and other features they observe in the process, may influence an individual's viewpoint on it.

For example, here are some questions my students have pursued in research into differing genres of televised text:

> How many close-ups occur in a quarter of a football game and what functions do they serve?
>
> How many women appear in a half-hour newscast as anchors, reporters, experts, victims, witnesses, and perpetrators, or others?
>
> How are problems resolved in a weekly episode of "Seinfeld"?

Each student fills in the following pre-research sheet.

Pre-Research Questionnaire

Name:_____ Date:_____

1. What genre of television content will you research? (sports, news, MTV, talk shows, etc.)

2. What is your research question? (Be sure your question is answerable by studying the content from the screen.)

3. What is your hypothesis? (What do you expect *now* that you will find?)

4. What are the categories of content that might need to be considered? (What *types* of functions do you believe this feature of the text deserves?)

5. Why do you think this kind of program is interesting?

6. Why do you think the feature of content you are studying is significant?

7. Do you anticipate any problems counting the number of times this feature occurs?

8. When do you plan to conduct your research? (What time is the program broadcast you want to analyze?)

I respond in writing to each of the proposals, perhaps narrowing the focus when a question is too broad to complete in a sitting or two. Depending upon the question, students develop appropriate coding (or counting) charts, which help them keep careful records of appearances of whatever feature is being tracked.

Close-Ups in Football Games

As a model research project, let's imagine Keith, who wants to research question number one: how many close-ups occur in one quarter of a football game and what functions do they serve? This is a quantifiable question. We define a *close-up* as any shot of an individual, shoulders up or tighter. Keith designs a coding chart so he can discriminate among persons in each close-up on screen as game play progresses. He creates columns or categories for players and coaches and fans and officials.

Keith watches the Detroit Lions play the Dallas Cowboys; his prior experience as a sports viewer helps him hypothesize about which players in this game will get the most screen time. Along with keeping track of discrete visuals, Keith is expected to copy down a few quotations from announcers, which he judges have an impact on how close-ups are perceived by viewers.

When Keith assembled his research data, he wrote a report, summarizing his findings, from which I quote here:

In this particular Monday night football game, Barry Sanders and
Emmit Smith were the most famous and well-known players As I
counted their close-ups (10 for Sanders and 8 for Smith out of 23
total), I realized that they had more than all the rest of the players
combined. Close-ups occurred during play of the game and also in
numerous replays that followed their strong runs. Sanders and Smith
got more replays than anybody else after their runs (at least 3 every
time) At the same time, commentators kept telling me how important these two were. Al Michaels said: "I tell you, you're watching
two of the best that ever played. No one could pick who's better."
But more than what he said was the way he said it. His tone of voice
played a big role in how much I wanted to see more of Sanders and
Smith. Subconsciously, I started to trust the commentators' analysts
more and more, because I was convinced they were helping me follow the most important people to watch.

With an exact count of close-ups in hand, Keith was struck by the power
of combined visual and verbal information to convince him of the
importance of two subjects. While this may seem obvious to sports fans, as
we extended the class conversation to talk about close-ups in other genres of
television text, the idea of how media create charismatic personalities came
to life (Morris 1994). Students saw how television creates and feeds viewers'
appetites to see the same people over and over again. In other words,
maximum presence increases expectation and attentiveness. Students
mentioned O. J. Simpson trial coverage as another example of this
phenomenon. We agreed that viewers' appetites for more information about
a media subject can increase when coverage is continuous and dramatic. An
athlete in the class adds to the observation about spin by saying that voice-
overs determine not just how important a person becomes, but what we
think about him or her:

The media can pump somebody up—and they talk about you as
good, people are looking at you that way, whether you are that good
or not. The media can talk bad about you, too. You can be out there
playing a great game, and the commentators say: This guy has a bad
attitude; he makes alot of mistakes. The viewer starts saying: He's
right; that guy doesn't want to win. But then, on the flip side, the
player is doing the very same thing, but the commentator says: This
player works hard every day. If you work hard, you can still make
mistakes, but he'll be back next game. Viewers then say: Hey, so
what, he just made a mistake. The media can make or break some
players that way. (Gordon and Morris 1993)

Through research group discussion, then, we begin to see not just how
often a feature appears on the screen, or why, but what sorts of factors, in

addition to an image, influence how we attribute cause or blame or relevance. Both counting the number of times close-ups occurred and thinking about what sorts of commentary accompany visuals helped students think critically about visual/verbal text.

Women in Newscasts

Another student, dealing with the second question above (how many women appear in a half-hour newscast as anchors, reporters, experts, victims, witnesses, and perpetrators, or others?), traced frequency of women on televised newscasts, using a chart to get an accurate count by gender in news stories, as women appeared on the screen. Students who do this sort of study must keep track of roles that people play in television. If, for example, women appear often in news stories, but always as victims, then the text promotes an expectation that they are not experts or reporters, only victims.

Problems Resolved in "Seinfeld"

Finally, some students do television research using other viewers by asking them to respond to content. In order to conduct what we call focus group research, they need to prepare viewer questionnaires, which are analyzed later, to study how different viewers read and react to the text. In the case of the third research question (how are problems resolved in a weekly episode of "Seinfeld"?) I helped Julie prepare a questionnaire (see Figure 2) that would yield information from her focus group by gender and by familiarity with the series.

In Julie's case, she assembled three family members and three friends; five of the six people try never to miss the show anyway. She asked them to fill in the A, B, and C categories before the show started, and then fill in the remaining D section either during or after the episode. She asked the focus group not to talk about the program until everyone had filled in the questionnaire. After she collected the questionnaires, she also led a discussion and copied down some notes about people's informal impressions of reasons for the program's overwhelming popularity with the viewing public.

When Julie wrote up her analysis of the questionnaires and the discussion afterward, she noted surprisingly little difference by gender in responses and was struck by everyone's appreciation for the character of George. In this particular episode, George was supposed to give a talk at work to New York Yankee higher-ups about Risk Management, a topic he had claimed on his

Viewer Response Questionnaire   **Date** _____

Your Name _____ Gender   M   F   (Circle one)

PLEASE DO NOT TALK DURING THE SCREENING OF "SEINFELD."

Complete B–C either on the basis of past experience or on the basis of this screening. Complete D as you watch now.

A. Have you ever watched "Seinfeld" before this screening?
     YES   NO   (Circle one)

B. Rank the program on the scale:
     Exceptional   Very Good   Good   Adequate   Poor

C. Which of the 4 characters do you rate as most compelling and/or interesting?

    Please rank from 1–4 in order of preference; One is your top ranking. Please provide:

    Jerry _____   _____ (one word descriptor)

    George _____   _____ (one word descriptor)

    Elaine _____   _____ (one word descriptor)

    Kramer _____   _____ (one word descriptor)

D. SUBPLOTS
    Each of the characters, each week, has a problem to solve. Together, the four characters discuss the problem, ways to solve it, and then reconsider the outcome of the attempts to find a solution.

    Watch the program; as you do, please fill in the following chart. Be specific and concise. Differences among viewers about conceptualizing problems and solutions are important to my research.

Figure 2. Viewer Response Questionnaire

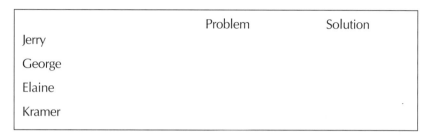

	Problem	Solution
Jerry		
George		
Elaine		
Kramer		

Figure 2. Continued

employment resume to be an expert in, but actually knew nothing about. As Julie's focus group laughed about George's dilemma and his bumbling attempts to get out of the presentation, Julie felt that viewers sympathized with him because so many employees today genuinely are afraid of being down-sized or fired. The predicaments George either gets himself into, or finds himself in, are bizarre, potentially threatening circumstances; Julie thought they could be associated with legitimate 1990s employment and security fears. Because our daily news is filled with stories of corruption and misuse of power in corporations, George is actually something of a trickster hero, a valiant finagler, who continually escapes a terrible fate, perhaps resembling a Chaplinesque figure.

Everyone in Julie's focus group remarked about and appreciated the high quality of the program's scripts and actors. Julie felt that "Seinfeld" humor was not only first rate but reflected greater public awareness of absurd everyday dilemmas, in all walks of life, which people see in the media, perhaps hear about on talk shows. In that regard, she considered the program a contemporary comedy, distinct from those of previous decades (such as the "Mary Tyler Moore" ensemble sitcom). In this way, Julie was venturing into cultural analysis, speculating that "Seinfeld" depicts a culturally desirable locale for the public, where characters laugh at themselves and each other, yet are not altogether undone by their human failings. Julie felt people hoped to find a similar community of loyal friends, however eccentric they are, to see them through, regardless of whatever happens.

Reporting Findings

In each of the cases described briefly here, students undertook a television research project, either employing strict content analysis or content analysis with focus group questions, assembling data to address a specific question, and, then, speculating about meanings of their findings with our class as a whole. Through oral presentations and discussions, the class deepened their personal and collective knowledge of text analysis. Each student submitted a report detailing her or his research as it was conducted and an interpretation, attaching coding sheets or questionnaires, and ultimately using this material to formulate an appropriate oral presentation, based on evidence gathered.

Language arts teachers, accustomed as they are to qualitative analysis, may find it strange to begin non-print media research by counting how many times a feature occurs, only later moving into more interpretive language. However, my teaching experience with television tells me that students benefit greatly from beginning with precise attention to text before attempting to make broader claims about its positive or negative qualities.

Conclusion

I conclude with an observation from a student who recently completed his report (and classroom discussion), analyzing numbers and kinds of questions raised and answered (or not answered) in an episode of "The X-Files," a program which has two FBI agents investigating unexplainable, usually paranormal, phenomena. Jeff chose to analyze two complete programs, and came up with the following conclusions:

> The findings on my totals chart were very surprising, and not at all what I had hypothesized before I began logging. Episode 1 supports my hypothesis that most of the program's questions would not be answered; only 16 of the 40 questions I discovered throughout the program were answered. Episode 2, however, directly contradicted this finding; of the 20 questions I thought were raised, all but 5 were resolved.
>
> Future research on numbers of questions raised and answered by the ends of more programs needs to be done. Still, I believe that alot is left to the viewer's imagination and that a problem-solving emphasis helps to explain "X-Files'" popularity. Also, people are pretty familiar with not being able to explain things in their lives, although not supernatural stuff, usually. As a loyal "X-Files" viewer, I may be responding to questions in the program differently than others would, so I need to do some focus group research too. In any case, I want to know more about reasons behind the show's popularity and possible effects on the viewing population.

I call readers' attention to the authoritative ease in Jeff's voice as he thinks and writes about a television program which has significance for him. For many students, opportunities to deal substantively and openly with images and narratives they gravitate toward on the TV screen frees them to compose with a combination of confidence and curiosity I want them to achieve as critical analysts and academic writers (Morris 1989).

Works Cited

Gordon, Marilyn and Barbra S. Morris. 1993. "Media Representations of Student Athletes: The Player as Subject and Observer." (unpublished paper).

Morris, Barbra S. 1994. "Authorship of Metaphoric Imagery in Live Television Sportscasts." *Images in Language, Media, and Mind.* Roy Fox, ed. Urbana, IL: National Council of Teachers of English.

———. 1993. "Two Dimensions of Teaching Television Literacy: Analyzing Television Content and Analyzing Television Viewing." *Canadian Journal of Educational Communication* 22.1: 37–45.

———. 1989. "The Television Generation: Couch Potatoes or Informed Critics?" *English Journal* 78.8: 35–41.

3 A Semester of Action Research: Reinventing My English Teaching through Technology

Nancy Traubitz

The deadening day-by-day routine of getting to school, getting through the day, getting to classes, getting home, grading papers, preparing lesson plans destroys teachers. We give up on education in order to survive the job of teaching. Research feels like one more task. Paradoxically, *action research* changes the way we teach, and it is much more vital to practicing teachers than to pre-service teachers and even trainers of teachers or scholars of education—who are the usual producers and consumers of educational research. As a teacher pressured into giving up on education in order to teach, I undertook action research to save my life—intellectually, professionally, and probably literally—and the fact that it almost did me in should not disguise another fact, that it enabled me to reinvent myself.

Reassessing Teaching Strategies

I took the first step in action research when I began consciously to reassess my teaching strategies. I sensed that average students were not benefiting from the wealth of new educational technology to the same extent that advanced students were. I knew from personal observation that my advanced students flourished in technology-enriched settings, that my disabled students and second language students were using technology to complete tasks and speed English language acquisition. At the same time,

Reprinted from *English Journal*, January 1998.

my average students seemed less involved, less interested in even simple applications like word processing their compositions.

I presumed, working from my own experience, that technology was a good thing. All English teachers had already found, or would find as soon as equipment became more widely dispersed, that technology is irresistible. But I was becoming aware that some outstanding English teachers dismissed information technology as outside the realm of English classes, even detrimental to the humanities. Then, about two years ago, perhaps after too many technological glitches in my own classroom, I began to wonder if technology really does support curriculum content. And if it does, how do we get technology into average level English classes? What strategies using technology appeal to students in English classes?

Formulating a Question and Collecting Data

By asking questions, I was already taking the second step in action research, formulating a question that when answered could change my own classroom practices. I mulled over the range of issues raised by my daily classroom experience until I eventually articulated one question: What strategies will broaden the application of technology to a wider group of students? I set out to collect data, the third step in action research, using student surveys, samples of student work, and a personal reflection journal.

At the same time I began to collect data, I also welcomed a pre-service teacher to my classes. Where I thought new teachers, let alone pre-service teachers, would get the skills experienced teachers have struggled so painfully to acquire, I don't know. Yet, new teachers, like advanced students, are supposed to be way ahead and willing to teach their computing skills to laggard classroom teachers caught in the technology revolution. I guess I thought anyone born after 1960 knows at birth how to use a computer, and my student teacher did give some credence to that charming myth. With little direction from me, he used an electronic grade book and computerized attendance-taking procedures. He also developed and taught technology-enriched instructional materials.

When schools acquire new technology, they don't acquire a new staff. Teachers already feeling threatened find themselves responsible for expensive but strange, noisy, space-devouring, maintenance-requiring, reportedly dangerous, chunks of plastic. In the best circumstances, flexible and knowledgeable master teachers seek out answers, find training, and help each other acquire the skills necessary to use the new tools. What made me so sure I could draw my average students into the technological revolution was the fact that I was surrounded by such teachers.

Initial Survey Results

At the beginning of the next semester, my student teacher and I surveyed our English classes. The survey results confirmed a number of my casual observations. Students in advanced classes had more access to computer equipment at home than students in average classes. Students who had computers available at home used computers more at school. Advanced students liked computers, were comfortable with computers, and used computers more often and in more different ways than average students. In the narrative portion of the survey and in interviews, average students expressed their willingness to use more and different technology. They expressed strong feelings that the technological revolution had left them behind, and they resented it.

Implementing Strategies

I agreed with these students and, within days, my student teacher and I took the final step in action research, implementing the strategies we had identified together. I developed lessons infusing curriculum content with technology. Teaching in a school that on paper has almost enough computers to allow every student to use a computer for every assignment, I explored strategies to encourage average students to use them. I believed, foolishly as it turned out, that in our new, richly endowed school, all students were assured of frequent, unrestricted access to computers. Technology became part of specific English assignments, especially in writing, but I also developed new ways to deliver traditional English course curriculum using e-mail and publication on the World Wide Web.

For instance, Web writing assignments had to be word processed, desktop publishing assignments required the use of graphics, group presentations demanded hypertext and other non-linear formats, researchers surfed the World Wide Web, assignments encouraged scanning text, using digital and video cameras. I offered bonus credit to anyone willing to use any of the technology available in school, at work, or at home. I hypothesized that if students who know about computers like computers and do higher level work, I should encourage students to use computers for as many assignments, and in as many ways as possible.

In our brand new high school serving 2,200 students, I campaigned to make the three computer labs of 28 machines each assigned to the English Department (and used primarily for writing classes) more available to the entire range of English classes. I managed to secure Internet access in one of these three English labs. I finagled funds to have all computers in the second of the three labs loaded with presentation software. When the English Department computer labs were not available, we used the computer labs designated for the business and math departments. Because many students worked as student assistants with individual teachers or in office settings where computers were available, I encouraged them to work on their English assignments whenever they had free time. Three weeks into the semester, students who had out-of-school jobs in which they used computers were completing compositions on their coffee breaks at work.

Student Response

Some of the terrible things I was warned would happen, did not happen. For example, given the opportunity to write beyond the writing lab setting, students wrote, but that opportunity to write in other settings did not lead to wasted time in the writing lab. They wrote during class lab time and before school and during school and after school and at home and at work and wherever they could find a computer. Of course, their promiscuous "writing around" led to the virus infection of our school network, our most serious problem.

Other terrible things I was warned would happen, did happen but did not turn out to be so terrible. Kids lost their disks, but they gladly bought new ones and took responsibility for the loss rather than blaming me. With more opportunities to explore other sources, students used more sources, and they did not always know how, or choose, to document those sources. When I pointed out students needed to give credit where credit was due, they never argued with me. Of course, I spent time trying to find or invent standard documentation format for the new sources they used, but that was part of the research. Kids did share their writing assignments, but I came to agree with them that such collaboration is often team work rather than plagiarism.

Difficulties Implementing Technology

During the semester I spent articulating, identifying, and implementing strategies which broadened the application of technology to a wider group of students, the most serious impediment was not lack of equipment but rather a complex intermix of issues clustering around staffing that raised more significant difficulties than my initial difficulty of getting the technology to the kids.

Access

Days into my research, I was embroiled in a turf war. Who gets access to the equipment? I wanted to find strategies to broaden the applications of technology to a wider group of students, yet I constantly ran up against the widely held perception that technology belongs in the school's Tech wing. When technology moves beyond Tech Ed, expect applications in math and science, not in English. The belief that even word processing is a luxury, a frill in English class, allowed but not required, showed up as frequently among teachers as among their students, and as frequently among English teachers as in the parent, business, and academic communities. After all, students are currently denied the use of computers in everything from AP exams to state-mandated writing competency tests.

The most bitter turf wars were fought right in the English Department. Teachers who perceived themselves as "writing" teachers demanded priority use of the writing labs. After the writing classes, the department writing labs could be used for a week by seniors completing college applications, and then for a few days by sophomores developing job resumes, but only during the time freshman writing classes crammed for the state's mandated paper-and-pencil writing test. I had to pull my classes off the computers whenever a "writing" teacher claimed his or her right to priority consideration. Of course, a different configuration of the English curriculum into less emphatic writing versus reading segments will help resolve such turf conflicts, but conflict over access to the equipment remained an issue.

Staff Support

Six weeks into the project, I was mired in conflict over shifting job descriptions. Even with both my student teacher and myself interacting with the 28 students in each class as they worked in the writing lab with technology-infused instructional material, we could not survive physically without help. We needed what is defined in our system as a composition assistant, a staff member assigned to support the writing curriculum. Basing their refusal on their own interpretation of their written job description, the composition assistants declined to assist in my classes. I did not teach a "writing" class. I taught genre-based senior English classes.

School system administrators encouraged me, as the department chair, to clarify the composition assistant job description in-house and to insist composition included the assignments generated by a technology-infused writing program. Trying to accomplish such clarification, I managed to precipitate a department rebellion. A major result of my research was the recognition that a serious hurdle facing the educational establishment is the clarification of job descriptions for the instructional support staff who assist classroom teachers in implementing technology-infused curriculum. Who defines what we mean by a composition assistant? As we come to use presentation software as well as word processing, what does a composition look like? When we are all linked by technology, what does "establish a definition in-house" mean? What activities can be defined as "supporting the writing curriculum"?

Training for Students and Staff

Is it the English teacher's responsibility to train students to use technology that enriches the writing curriculum? As I mentioned above, students are often presumed to know how to use technology. In fact, they often know little more than how to play a video game. Occasionally students, supported by parents who see new technology as threatening their own work situations, simply refuse to use technology for any purpose. Then what happens to their English grade? Although I was willing to risk making myself look foolish for the sake of making technology more widely available to students, I was concerned with training issues, both for students and for staff.

What is an English teacher supposed to know and do? For example, given the fact that many university and public libraries no longer have card catalogues, should English teachers be allowed to formulate department policy requiring students to turn in note cards and bibliography cards? New technology has staffing implications.

In another instance, who is responsible for training users of the imaging technology and other equipment becoming available to the school publications housed in the English Department and supervised by English teachers? The frequent complaint that training is not available or that staff is expected to manage technology beyond or outside their assignment is balanced by the frequent refusal of staff to participate in training, even when training is provided on-site and during working hours.

System Malfunction

Of course, every training issue is complicated and doubled when the school uses a wide variety of networked equipment. I heard often, "You'll mess up the network and wipe out the whole department!" And I did. Responsibility for the well-being of the technology becomes more complex as we move beyond the physical vandalism of equipment to electronic sabotage. Exactly what virus and to what extent the computers assigned to the English Department were infected, I will never know. Why we were operating over a hundred networked computer work stations without any virus protection when we hold a systemwide site license for a good commercial protection system, I will never know. However, the writing labs and teachers' classroom work stations went down, at least to the extent that all student use of the equipment stopped. Looking over my data, I discover that at this point I stopped keeping a reflection journal. I still cannot bear to reflect on some of the behaviors and verbal exchanges of that week.

When the system goes down, who fixes it and when? This blurring of responsibility leads to frequent chaos. I planned the most exciting instructional opportunity for my students only to find the network down or the World Wide Web inaccessible. Machines broke down and languished unrepaired for weeks at a time.

Teachers are used to interruptions like snow days and fire drills. However, when the network fails, paranoia breaks out in the staff and boredom in the student body. Students and teachers grow reluctant to experiment when the technology fails repeatedly. Even if it doesn't fail frequently, a single failure leads to the perception that technology is excessively fragile.

Communication Problems

I was especially troubled by communication issues. Because I was trying something different, I struggled to keep my colleagues and my students informed. I used e-mail, I learned how to attach files, I even sent hard copy. Not a single colleague asked how my research was going, not one commented on the survey forms or read any of the survey results. However, we had shouting matches in the English office over the damage I was doing to the English program. E-mailers flamed me for the amusement of a staff of two hundred colleagues. What does *confidential* mean in a networked school? Who is responsible for teaching—and for practicing—netiquette? Can staff be required to read their e-mail?

Fortunately for me, both action research and technology implementation systemwide brought together groups of people experiencing the same stress and the same need for support and reassurance. Colleagues outside my own department and beyond my own school shared my concerns and were interested in the strategies I was developing for average students. Happily, recognition of the need for and the value of mutual support is a major outcome of my experience.

Classroom Management

And then, there were classroom management issues. I wrote elaborate day-by-day, minute-by-minute, step-by-step instructions, and still I spent too much class time going over plans and giving instructions. I finally taped daily instructions to the work table, the classroom board, and my back, and students still complained they never knew what they were doing. Infusing technology into English classes led to student behavior easily perceived as "off the wall," to student-teacher interactions that felt like and probably were beyond teacher control. Traditional classroom decorum melted away.

Was I doing the right thing in training my student teacher to tolerate such unstructured student behavior? What did this new classroom configuration look like to an administrator doing a formal observation? As the department chair, I had always tried to model the behaviors we had agreed upon as a department. Now I worried about making and enforcing spur-of-the-moment rules for the use of and behavior in technological settings like writing labs. I had to confront new issues raised by electronic plagiarism, develop and teach documentation format for electronic sources.

Final Student Survey

As the semester drew to a close, my student teacher finished his training and returned to his college program. I reclaimed my classes and, to the surprise of no one, administered another survey. Since completing my initial survey, all my students had used the graphic program in the word processing package to embellish a composition about symbolism and searched on-line dictionaries to write a composition-length logical definition. They had visited the home pages of their favorite music groups, downloading song lyrics from the home pages as part of a composition in which they compared a traditional English poem with a contemporary song lyric. They had surfed the

World Wide Web visiting South Africa and major legal repositories to research social issues related to their study of Alan Paton's novel *Cry, the Beloved Country.* As part of a group study of a novel set in Asia, they had published group web pages consisting of a digital image of an Asian artifact in our school collection, an information essay based on the research about the artifact found in print and electronic sources including the Web, and a creative writing segment. (These web pages are available as part of the school's home page at: www.mcps. k12. md.us/schools/springbrookhs/.) Yet, when I asked students if they had grown more comfortable using technology, half insisted they had never been allowed to use the Web and did not know the meaning of the word *graphic.*

At the close of the school year, in the rush of graduation rehearsal, I asked these students for narrative input, both in journal notes and in another survey. Students and statistics agreed that class attendance had improved. Class attentiveness and retention of information increased, although the classroom and writing lab never returned to a quiet, orderly environment. Grades improved markedly, and students actually admitted to enjoying the work and feeling better about their ability to do the assignments. More significantly, students who had been academically uninvolved voiced a determination to complete their technologically-enriched projects. Several students, who had insisted they would not/could not graduate, set up individual contracts with me to make up work missed earlier in the semester. Not a single student failed or lost credit for the last quarter of the semester.

In my increasing awareness of the role of a support team for teachers willing to undertake such research, I also informally surveyed staff members who had worked with me during the web page project. These colleagues included the English Department instructional assistant, the media center staff, the guidance office staff, and a department colleague also engaged in action research. We agreed the students' increased self-confidence and self-esteem was due partly to their imminent graduation but also to the attention their web pages received.

Conclusion

Fortunately for me, both action research and technology implementation systemwide brought together groups of people experiencing the same stress and the same need for support and reassurance. Colleagues outside my own department and beyond my own school shared my concerns and were interested in the strategies I was developing for average students. Recognition of the need for and the value of mutual support is a major outcome of my experience.

Thanks to my action research, I may actually be a better teacher next year. However, I set out to find answers and found, instead, more questions. I sought solutions and found, instead, untested strategies. I hoped for results and found, instead, only process. The issues I stumbled over as I struggled to broaden the application of technology have not been resolved. I do believe they can be resolved, though, and that they are being resolved through a process of reinvention, the reinventing of our teaching and of our profession.

4 Bridging the Gap: Integrating Video and Audio Cassettes into Literature Programs

Kay Beth Avery, Charles W. Avery, and Debra Partin Pace

For students who seldom read, understanding the meaning of the words on the page and the rhetorical devices within them are two separate skills, too difficult to master simultaneously. Then how do teachers introduce style and literary techniques to average students, many of whom are reluctant readers and many of whom come from culturally diverse backgrounds where English is a second language? How do we teach them to see and feel the symbols, themes, and archetypes in classical novels? Students with underdeveloped linguistic abilities may be unwilling or unable to unravel the mysteries of a long book. Yet, what these students cannot see on the printed page they can more readily recognize in other media. Adolescents who grew up listening to countless hours of television and radio are already comfortable with movies and audio cassettes. Doesn't it seem reasonable that many of these students might be more able to analyze complex ideas that are first introduced via visual and audio adaptations of a literary work?

Of course, no self-respecting English teacher wants to be accused of watering down the curriculum by showing a movie simply to fill two hours of class time or in order to divert students from reading the actual novel. The challenge, then, is to enable students to go beyond an appealing movie story line into more complex examinations of themes, symbols, and literary technique by building a bridge to the printed text. The specific teaching

Reprinted from *English Journal*, February 1998.

strategies will vary, depending upon the teacher's preferences and the students' abilities. However, below are just a few of the possible activities that can accompany a video and/or audio cassette.

Activities to Bridge the Gap

Stimulate Reading by Allowing Students to Listen to an Audio Cassette of the Novel as They Follow Along Silently in Copies of the Text

At the end of several days of read-a-long and accompanying activities, show the students the film adaptation of the book. Encourage students to point out the similarities and differences between the book and movie. The common approach used by teachers in the past was to assign silent reading of the entire novel and then show the film. However, this traditional approach serves as a meager and unsatisfying reward for reluctant readers who need the additional auditory stimulus to understand and appreciate even short, "high interest" novels, much less classical literature.

Teachers can purchase commercial, unabridged audio versions of many books. If a commercial version doesn't exist, teachers can create their own or enlist the aid of drama students. Some advanced students may be willing to create an audio cassette of one or two action-packed chapters as a required project or for extra credit.

For an example, teachers might require a class of students to read along to the entire text of *Of Mice and Men*. On the other hand, teachers may choose to read only a single chapter excerpt from *The Great Gatsby* or may even have to create their own recordings of episodes from *The Natural*.

Show Only the Beginning of the Movie or an Exciting Excerpt to Contextualize the Work and to Introduce the Major Characters

This strategy is particularly effective for psychological novels and period classics with slow-moving plots and complicated historical backgrounds. Showing all but the last 30 minutes of a movie also triggers the curiosity of students who are then motivated to read the last few chapters of a classic. Even average readers have been known to plod their way through the final chapters of Edith Wharton's *Age of Innocence* or *Ethan Frome* in order to find the answer to the question they so vehemently asked at the end of a class period, "How does it end? That's not fair! Come on, please show us how it ends!"

Take Students on a Field Trip to See the Latest Remake of an Old Classic

For example, the newest version of *The Scarlet Letter* (1995, Dir. Roland Joffe, Hollywood Pictures), with Demi Moore and Robert De Niro, played in movie theaters across the country within the 1995–96 school year. *The Literary Cavalcade* (September 1995) devoted ten pages to a shortened version of the screenplay in an article that highlighted differences between the movie script and Nathaniel Hawthorne's original. A teacher might begin the unit by having students read this article (perhaps out loud as a class). The next day the class reads the opening chapters of the novel (assisted perhaps by the tool of an audio cassette read-a-long, available for purchase for about $20). The teacher then leads a discussion reviewing the startling contrasts between these chapters and the movie version. Students are told that their final test over the unit will be a comparison essay evaluating the differences between the book and the movie.

Those students who cannot go on the field trip can rely on the *Literary Cavalcade* article, which recaps the entire plot of the screenplay. However, all students will have to read the book in order to discover some major differences between the last half of the book and the last half of the movie.

Jigsaw the Reading of a Novel So That Students in Small Groups Are Dependent upon Each Other for Answers; Then Show the Movie

Divide the class into small groups with three members to a group. Group member number one of each group reads the first third of the novel. Group member number two reads the middle portion. The third group member reads the last third of the book. Tell students that their mission is not impossible, but it does involve the solving of a mystery: they must work together to unravel the plot of the novel. Allow time in class for silent reading so that each individual can complete his portion of the novel.

An alternate method for getting students through their required third of the novel is a paired reading technique. With paired reading two students assigned the same section of the book read together. (Often a good reader is paired with a slower reader.) The first member of the pair reads a page or two of text aloud. Then the pair of students work together to write a short statement summarizing the main action on that page. Group member number two now reads a page of text aloud. This switching of roles continues until the entire passage is completed. Pairs that read quietly without disturbing other groups, remain on task, and complete a list of events for their section of the novel receive a good grade for the day.

Incidentally, this paired reading also insures a checking for accuracy of information before the small groups meet to complete the jigsaw. During Phase Two, within the small groups composed of three students, each group member is responsible for relaying a description of the events within his/her third of the novel. The mission of the entire group is to complete a sequence chain or a list that outlines the action of the entire novel. Now the teacher can show the film adaptation as a means of review.

For this unit, one appropriate assessment of student learning is the plot summary, requiring each student to pick out the most important events of the movie and to organize them into one unified, eight- to ten-sentence paragraph.

Introduce Symbols and through Class Discussion Assist Students to Interpret Symbolism

Pose a probing question and have students brainstorm answers as the teacher or a student volunteer records answers on the blackboard. For example, to study symbols, the question set for the day might read:

A) What is a symbol?

B) What symbols can you find in this room or in this school?

C) What are some other common symbols that you see every day in the real world?

D) What are some symbols you remember from books you've read in the past?

E) What symbols can you find in this particular movie?

Place one question at a time on the blackboard or overhead transparency. Fill up the blank space with student responses, using the inquiry method, withholding judgment and teacher comments until the blackboard is full.

If a class were examining the film adaptation of Bernard Malamud's *The Natural,* the following are some of the symbols that might wind up on the blackboard:

- The gambler in the story uses an evil eye to unveil the secrets of his victims.
- The judge, who represents the corruption and mire of underworld finance, keeps his office dark and gloomy.
- Harriet and Memo, representing decadence and evil, dress predominantly in black while Iris, the pure and faithful, dresses predominantly in white.

- Two other symbols, lightning and Roy's bat, emphasize nature as a driving force and the driving force in Roy. When fate and the gods are on his side, Roy is a lightning rod and super hero rising above corruption and mortal frailties. Each time Roy hits a crucial home run, lightning or a cascade of lights accompanies the act.

Compare Two Key Concepts or Two Key Symbols

Show students how to pair key words together by providing a couple of examples and then assigning cooperative groups different pairs of key words. For instance, a cooperative study group examining the film, *The Natural* (1984, Dir. Barry Levinson, Tri-Star), may pair "Wonder Boy" and the "Savoy Special" while another group is assigned Memo and Harriet.

The first cooperative group draws a circle picturing a lightning rod on a bat and a second circle illustrating a bat on which has been engraved the words "Savoy Special." Under Circle Number One the group writes: *power, lightning strength natural talent, Roy's essence, made by Roy,* and *Roy's craftsmanship.* Under Circle Number Two the group places these phrases: *more powerful and stronger, new talent, passing the baton, handcrafted by the young water boy,* and *Roy's giving of himself to the next generation.* The group assigned Harriet and Memo considers several similarities and differences in these two women. Allow time at the end of the period for groups to explain their drawings to the whole class.

Analyze Theme and Characterization

Generate lists by categories on a graphic organizer through class discussion. (Record answers on an overhead transparency so students can copy them and refer to them later when writing essays.)

To model the use of graphic organizers label the three circles of a modified Venn diagram, three columns of a comparison chart, or three boxes on a power map with the following three subtopics: symbols, themes, and characters. Using the inquiry method, allow students to fill in the details. For a less complex comparison, choose three characters. Each character becomes a main subtopic. Insure depth in the supporting details by preparing a battery of questions that students can answer on each character:

- What color is most important in describing this character?
- What are the mood and feelings associated with this character?

- Describe the character's personality.
- List at least three important statements made by this character.
- What are the most important actions and reactions of this character?
- What else is important about the character?

The chart below, geared to a study of *The Natural,* is another example of an appropriate graphic organizer for analyzing characters.

Name	Desires	Deeds	Dramatic Quotes
Roy	Wanted to be the best	Uses a bat and ball to try to achieve that power	He wants "to be the best there ever was in the game."
	Lusted after Memo, glory, and fame	Abandoned Iris and started dating Memo	He is going where he will "be the champ and have what goes with it."

Note that while some of the activities have been illustrated through a film adaptation, they can just as easily be used to teach meaning within the actual text. However, many teachers may use a symbol-laden movie like *The Natural* as an entity complete unto itself, a legitimate introduction to literary devices. Then once students see the complex, yet obvious, symbols in this movie, they can more clearly recognize them in other works. For instance, teaching a comparison between *The Great Gatsby,* the movie, and *The Great Gatsby,* the novel, is made easier by the insight students gain through exposure to *The Natural's* heavy-handed use of symbols.

Relate Literature to the Real World by Motivating Students to Defend Their Opinions on Current Social Issues

Spend a class period asking the question, "What's the message this book and/or movie brings to modern man (or modern woman)?" For example, many students who view the 1984 film adaptation of *The Natural* choose to discuss deterioration of the family unit. Iris and Roy's son pay a dear price for Roy's success. While Roy wanders aimlessly in the midst of depression and self-pity for sixteen years, Iris and the son must learn to cope without a husband and father. Upon meeting with Iris after sixteen years, Roy grants that "a father can make all the difference." For Roy's son, as for the children of today, a mother and father, working harmoniously together, can make all the difference.

When "Wonder Boy" (Roy's bat) cracks under pressure, it is natural that the "Savoy Special" should take its place. The creation and destruction of "Wonder Boy" marks the beginning and the end of Roy's career in professional baseball. This polished stick of wood is his craftsmanship, his talent, his essence, all rolled into one. As if he were passing the baton, the "Savoy Special" signifies the coming of a new generation.

Encourage Reflection through Journal Entries

After students discuss the work's relevance to their world, ask students to write about these connections. A high school student describes one lesson in simple terms: "In a wide open field, Roy teaches his boy how to play ball, just like his father did with him. Roy realizes that it is not important to be the best there ever was but to be true to himself." According to this student, Roy learns to give some of himself to the next generation. Roy begins his journey of initiation with the sole dream of personal glory and ends his journey realizing that he must give to others: his teammates, his wife, and his son.

Link the Themes in a Film or Book to Themes in Other Important Literary Works

The Natural provides multiple opportunities to tie a film to other important literary works. Roy's journey toward self-realization connects with Huck Finn's exploration of civilization along the banks of the Mississippi and Gene's coming of age in *A Separate Peace*.

Roy's identity crisis is also reminiscent of Richard Wright's search for self in *Black Boy*. Roy's drift into big league baseball and his return to the simple priorities of the farm reflect the nurturing power of nature, a theme echoing from the writings of the Romantics, such as Thoreau and Wordsworth. Roy's willful pride in his ability and selfish determination to be "the best" also parallel that of ancient Greek heroes, such as that of Achilles in *The Iliad*. Long lists of examples can be organized into two column notes, such as those following.

Subtopics	Supporting Details
Huckleberry Finn	Huck is like Roy because both are trying to understand how to relate to the society in which they live.
A Separate Peace	Both Gene and Roy come of age as they struggle to let go of old goals and reevaluate new friendships.
Black Boy	Richard and Roy both search for their own identities and for new approaches to building self-worth.
Walden	Both Roy and Henry David Thoreau value individual worth and nature. Both discover the healing power of nature.

Study Significant Dialogue

Ask cooperative groups to create storyboards on which cartoon or stick figures speak memorable dialogue from the film or novel. Pull out the colored pencils, magic markers, and crayons and stimulate spatial and tactile learning by integrating art into the English classroom. Twenty dollars of supplies goes a long way toward creating both fun and motivation, even in secondary school.

Prior to viewing the movie, students are asked to jot down memorable quotations. Then after seeing all or part of it, students are divided into groups. Each group needs a recorder of the words to be used in the script, an organizer or clarifier to lay out the order of events, and an artist to draw the script, or all group members can assume all roles.

Post these student products on the classroom walls and refer to them when discussing related lessons. In fact, any of the student products described in this article can be generated on poster board or butcher paper so that they can be displayed on the walls of the classroom and easily shared with the entire class. If time permits, allow students to practice and present their new storyboards as skits.

Integrate Several Strategies into One Unit

Teach to multiple intelligence levels by appealing to all five senses. For example, a teacher might choose to use professionally recorded audio cassettes for *Of Mice and Men,* having students read along to two chapters at the beginning of each class period until the novel is completed. The second half of each period is then devoted to motivating activities related to the subject matter in that particular chapter. One day students work in groups to create and act out skits that dramatize a particular episode. Another day they relate the theme in a poem by Robert Frost about two tramps to the characters in the novel. On still another day, students analyze harmful stereotypes and generalizations found throughout the novel, using fairly complex logic and analysis to connect statements in the novel to intrapersonal experiences. Then they draw a character and write a short summary of his or her strengths and weaknesses. Finally, they create a song that summarizes the main characters and themes in the novel.

Conclusion

Movies in the English classroom are more than fillers or emergency lesson plans, in spite of the misuse and "bad rep" with which they are sometimes associated. Video and audio cassettes should not replace the written word, but they can serve as helpful tools for building bridges over the chasm of confusion and lack of interest felt by reluctant readers. Every age, even ours, is blessed with bookworms willing to read almost anything. However, many of today's high school students need assistance winding their way through difficult literature. For these students, audio and film adaptations can improve reading comprehension and open doors to the rhetorical devices locked within the text of a good book.

II Second Language Learners

Teaching students whose first language is not English is a challenge that faces teachers from all content areas. However, because language is the medium and the content of the English language arts classroom, English language arts teachers often bear the responsibility for English as a Second Language students' growth in all content areas. ESL classes are often available to students, but as Danling Fu points out, many parents do not want their children in these classes because of real or perceived decontextualized and unmeaningful instruction.

Fu joins the other writers of this section in calling for instruction that engages students as they develop English literacy. Students need to be immersed in reading, writing, and speaking that draws upon their primary culture and facilitates growth in English. Mary Kooy and Annette Chiu emphasize the importance of literature in this process. They feel that authentic reading instruction has been downplayed to the detriment of the ESL student.

Miles Gullingsrud and Anne Fairbrother address the issues of second language learners and multicultural populations in general in holistic and specific ways. They highlight the importance of the teacher's vigilant awareness of baggage stemming from his or her own race and ethnicity, while addressing students as individuals and members of a cultural group.

5 Unlock Their Lonely Hearts

Danling Fu

Thirteen years ago, when I boarded the airplane to America (the literary translation from Chinese is the Beautiful Country), I thought I was going to heaven on earth. Many people in China thought so, too. They envied me. Soon after I arrived, however, I realized that my new life in this totally strange land was much harder than the life I lived through during my teenage years in China when I was sent to work on a farm, a primitive life when compared to the living conditions in America. Life in America made me fundamentally understand that material life is not everything. A good life to a person means more than material needs. Coming to this country, I had to leave all my family and everything I knew behind. The loss and alienation I was confronted with every day caused tremendous pain in the first few years of my life in this country.

Reading the writing by new Chinese immigrant children in a Chinatown middle school in New York, I found that they were suffering the same trauma I went through. In their writing, they wrote about how much they missed their grandparents, their cousins, their friends, their houses, and their villages. Some expressed grief and loneliness. Rui Huang, an eighth grader, painted a colorful heart and wrote:

> This picture is about a heart which is a person who have lots of colors, means this person have lots of things to think and lots of bad stuff happen to this person but too bad this person have nobody to talk too. This person is a very lonely person who is like lock up to a cave or a cage.

Rui painted a wounded heart, filled with loneliness and isolation. It is a very sad heart. Between the lines, I felt the loss, the pain, and the feelings of

Reprinted from *Voices from the Middle*, September 1998.

dislocation. This sadness permeates the pages of so many new Chinese immigrant youngsters' writing. Even though, as far as material needs are concerned, their lives in America are much better than they were in China, they all expressed a strong wish to go back to China.

For the first two years of my living in America, I wanted to go back to China every day. Today, it is the American literacy I have gained that has become my bridge to American culture, and linked me more and more with this country and its people. As a literate person in this world, I have finally found my place in this English-speaking country and feel this land is my home.

Seeing new immigrant children suffer the same trauma I went through, I feel my role as educator is to help ease their pain and to facilitate their transition to this new land. From my own experience, I know the sooner they learn to communicate with others in English and enter the American literacy, the better they will feel about their part in this new world. Literacy education is the key to initiating them into American culture, to helping them feel this country is their home, and to unlocking their lonely hearts.

Working as a monthly consultant in a middle school in New York's Chinatown, I have realized once again that there is no unified formula in teaching. As ESL students, Chinese immigrant children in Chinatown presented unique situations and learning patterns that were quite different from what I had learned from my research, my own learning experiences as an ESL student, and my previous work with ESL learners. Studying, working, thinking, and re-examining our practices in these special circumstances with a group of dedicated teachers, staff developers, and administrators have deepened my understanding of many issues related to the teaching of ESL students and bilingual and literacy education.

"How comes he still can't speak a word of English?!"

One day in March, a parent of an eighth-grade student, holding her son's composition written in Chinese, came to the teacher and cried out, "My child came to the school since last September. Now it is March. How comes he still can't speak a word of English? How comes?! What happens?" During my first visit as a consultant to this middle school, I was as shocked as this parent. I saw many children who could barely speak any English after having been in the school for two or three years, a few even for seven years. As a language teacher, an ESL learner, and a parent of a bilingual child myself, I was dumbfounded. But I realize now that the children living in Chinatown have a limited English language environment. To them, English is more a foreign language than a second language. Chinatown provides them everything in Chinese: shopping, TV, newspapers, and books. They seldom leave Chinatown to see other parts of New York City. Chinatown is an extension of China to them.

Even at school, with a student population that is 85% Chinese, they don't need to speak much English. Peers speak Chinese in and out of class (including working on class projects in group activities). Teachers, although largely native speakers of English, respect their students' home culture and first language, and don't feel like pushing their students to speak English. Rather, many of them try hard to learn Chinese in order to understand and communicate with their students better. I found some native-English-speaking teachers trying harder to speak Chinese than their students do to speak English. In this school, Chinese is definitely not seen as a language inferior to English, unlike in many other American schools.

However, the students' inefficiency and slow development in English language learning worry many teachers, parents, administrators, and the students themselves. Many students want to leave the ESL program so they can speak more English. They are afraid that they will never be able to get into good high schools or any colleges. Everyone knows, including students themselves, that English is the key for these children to enter the real American world.

"How much Chinese do we allow them to speak in class?"

Our educational aims and goals are to help these children gain equal opportunity in American society, so we first must help these students acquire proficiency in English and initiate them into American literacy. Providing more opportunities for the students to communicate in English (listening and speaking) is our first goal. But this doesn't mean we forbid the use of the first language in school. As Krashen (1996) states: "'English only' rules are not good for English. Peer help should be done the same way we do it in bilingual education programs: As a source of background information and academic knowledge in the first language, not as on-line translation" (p. 14).

The challenge we face is how to push these students to use English as much as possible in their learning, but at the same time maintain our respect for their first language and home culture. At a faculty meeting, when we emphasized the importance of English speaking for our students, we encountered questions like these: "How much Chinese do we allow them to speak in class?" "How can I ask these Chinese children to speak out, especially the girls, when they are not encouraged to express their ideas openly in their own culture?" To deal with this perplexity, we examined the essence of "respect students' first language and home culture."

We believe that as teachers, we need to respect our children's home culture and language, but not at the expense of losing their educational opportunity. To respect our students' home culture and language posits that their culture and language are not inferior to the mainstream culture and language, and that it holds equal value to any other cultures. Their home cultural experience and first language literacy is the bridge and resource for their second language learning in a new literacy. Only when what a student possesses or knows can serve as the foundation for new learning can he or she become confident in exploring a new language. To respect students' culture and language in American literacy education doesn't mean keeping students in an environment identical to the one in which they were raised, but rather helping them grow and form their new identity in a new culture. To respect their home culture doesn't mean we have to accept every belief that culture holds. Every culture has its beauty but also its faults. Some cultures believe girls are not as valuable as boys, or that adults and children don't share equal rights. Do we have to encourage the children who come from that culture to hold onto these beliefs? Is this the way to respect their culture? My grandma would never imagine a woman like me could leave home and go to another country to pursue her education. I am glad that I am able to do many things that my grandma and mother were not allowed to do in their generations. Every culture has moved along with the progress of the world.

In American education, we educate Chinese immigrant children not just to be Chinese, but to be Chinese-Americans. When we introduce them to a new language, to a new literacy, at the same time, we open them to a set of new values and a new world. We are preparing them for what they came here for: to be Chinese-Americans in this country. When a mother waved a composition her child wrote in Chinese for an English class saying, "I don't want my son to learn to write in Chinese, I want him to learn to write in English," she didn't mean to demean the Chinese language, but cried "Please prepare him for this English-speaking world." When the Chinese children requested a transfer from the bilingual program, it was not because they didn't appreciate their home language, but because they wanted a more vigorous program where education would be more like that of other children around the country.

If we think that speaking helps these children to learn language and literacy, we should encourage them and provide them with opportunities to do so, but we also need to understand why it is hard for them, especially for some girls, to speak up, and why they need more time, courage, and practice. We shouldn't assume that what comes easy for us, or for American students, should also come easy for these students. That is the essential meaning of "respect our students' culture and language."

"Please give them more work and help them learn more English!"

At a parent meeting, when we asked the parents to help us educate their children, many of them pleaded with us, "Please give them more work and help them learn more English! We don't know English, we don't know how to help them. But they listen to the teachers, they will do whatever you ask them to do. Please assign them more homework." Their pleas underscore their desire for and their anxiety about their children's education. Parents can tell that their children are far behind others of their age in this country and lack the literacy they need to function here. The adults suffer from being illiterate in this English-speaking country; they don't want this to happen to their children.

Many people tend to think, although research does not prove it, that the students who lack the basic language skills must grasp them before they can speak, read, and write for real purposes. During my first visit to this middle school, I observed a seventh-grade ESL English class. For the first half hour, the teacher had her students practice writing the letter "A." While the students were writing, she circulated from seat to seat to check their work. I sat next to a boy in the back row and watched him write "A" at least 50 times. Then he started to draw while waiting for the teacher to come to his seat. When she finally came to him, she found that he didn't do the work in the exact way she had directed. She asked him to erase all he did and rewrite the letter "A" five times, which only took him ten seconds. After the teacher checked all the students, she went to the front. I thought that she would have her students do something more exciting for the remaining 20 minutes. Surprisingly, she took out another worksheet and said to the class: "Let's practice writing the letter 'B.'" I couldn't stand this anymore and left the room. I felt sorry for those students, as they had to stay through what was intolerable for me and had to do obediently whatever they were asked to do.

Maybe these seventh-grade students do need to practice writing 26 alphabetic letters. But isn't it wasteful and boring to spend the whole class period practicing two of them? With this kind of teaching, how much can these children learn in a year? How soon will they start to speak some English? I have visited many kindergarten classrooms, but I have never seen a class spend such a long time practicing writing alphabetic letters. No wonder some students who have been in this country for three years still can't speak much English!

Their parents have sacrificed a lot for these children. They work day and night at odd hours for minimum wage. Many of them have to hold several jobs or change jobs frequently to make ends meet. They left the land where they were born and raised, and came here so their children could have a better education and life than they had in China. They trust that if they work hard and their children study hard at school, their American dream will come true. Trueba, Lila, and Kirton (1990) state:

> [N]o one is willing to pay a higher price [than the immigrants and refugees] in order to achieve the American dream. Therefore, they endure hardships and drastic social and cultural changes unbearable for others, and they buy into American ideals of social, economic and political participation, and of educational opportunity equally accessible to all (p. 1).

Are we providing these Chinese immigrant children equal educational opportunity and helping them make their dreams come true when we give them work that no intelligent person could stand?

ESL teachers are not teaching only basic English skills or functional literacy (simply for survival). We have a more challenging job than many of our colleagues, just as our ESL students encounter more challenging learning in the English-speaking world than their counterparts. We are not just preparing our students to transfer to mainstream programs; we want to initiate them into American literacy, and open them to all the opportunities this democratic country can offer to its people. We need to help them realize their dreams and usher them into a new world full of possibilities. We are the ones who, through our everyday teaching, make our students understand the value of the sacrifices they and their families have made, and that what they want to achieve in this land is possible. We are initiating them into the American literacy, which is the key to unlocking their lonely hearts. This is not an easy job, and it shouldn't be boring; we can't afford to waste any time. Whether these children will feel America is their new home, whether they will love this country, whether they will make it in this new land lies on our shoulders.

A recently arrived student wrote in her journal:

> I like China, because in China, everyone speak Chinese, I can under-
> stand. But in America, American people all speak English. I don't
> understand. If I can speak English, I like America too. Now [my] wish
> is I can speak English. Because I like America too. So, I must learn
> English.

How can an educator not be touched by this student's wish and will?
Therefore, to challenge ourselves in teaching and learning is to constantly
ask ourselves: Does our everyday teaching contribute to our students' future
success in this world? Is every activity we design significant and meaningful
enough for our students' present life now? Do I really respect my students'
intelligence?

"We want harder work and learn more English."

One day, three girls marched to the assistant principal's office requesting to
leave the ESL program, which they felt was "too easy." "We want harder
work and learn more English. If we stay this way, we will never go to a good
high school and never get into a college." The children wanted to be
challenged, and they were not pleased with only learning basic skills. Can
they read and write to communicate to others and express themselves before
they master the English skills? Teachers of every grade in this school
demonstrated this possibility, including a brand new young teacher,
Kimberly Wertzel.

Kimberly had 21 recently arrived students. They had been in this country
anywhere from a few days to two or three months. None of them could
speak much English, and some could read and write very little in English.
Kimberly read to her students every day and provided them with plenty of
opportunities to speak, read, and write. From day one when these students
came to this class, they were encouraged to use as much English as possible.

They had time to write every day. When they couldn't write in English,
they wrote in Chinese. In this class, the students' writing demonstrated their
English learning at different stages: some could only write in Chinese, some
wrote in Chinese mixed with some English words and phrases, some
expressed themselves in half Chinese and English, some wrote all in English
but in Chinese syntax and expressions (Chinese-English), and some started to
write close to standard English (see Figure 1).

Figure 1. Students' writing at the different stages in English learning

In their writing, these newly arrived youngsters expressed their vivid memories of their home country, the friends and relatives they left behind, and the houses and villages where they used to live. They also expressed their fear, their loneliness, their new experience in this new culture, and their wonders, questions, and wishes for this new world.

In teaching them English, Kimberly helped her students express what they had to say and wanted to know. They did start to write and speak in Chinese when their English was not proficient enough. The students worked in pairs and groups to practice English speaking, reading, and writing. As time went on, they used more and more English in their speaking and writing. So, again, how much Chinese can we allow them to speak in class if we need to push them to speak as much English as possible? To answer this question is like answering these: How long should we let our children use inventive spelling? How long should we let our babies speak telegraphic language? How long should we let them crawl? This ESL teacher demonstrated the same answer to all these questions: push them to the edge constantly. As soon as these Chinese children could speak one English word, she provided them with opportunities to practice speaking it and writing it in meaningful contexts.

Like Kimberly, some other English and science teachers have proved that to challenge students is not to give them tons of difficult work, but to discover their possibilities and push them to their full potential. If the students can do the work by themselves, we shouldn't use class time for it. If the students can do the work in two minutes, we shouldn't spend twenty minutes on it. To challenge them is to respect their intelligence and to acknowledge their capacity and individuality.

"Grab onto anyone to practice English speaking."

One day in an eighth-grade science class, a girl came to Maureen, a staff developer, trying hard to tell her, "I want to learn how to speak English better. But in Chinatown, every one speaks Chinese, I can't have opportunity to speak English. My mom told me to grab onto anyone to practice English speaking." Her words reminded me of my own experience when I studied English in China—little opportunity for listening to and speaking English. What a shame that right in this English-speaking world, these students feel the same way as those outside the country. This immigrant girl's burning desire and frustration tell us that we haven't done enough for our students and our teaching hasn't satisfied their thirst for knowledge.

Among all the language skills, speaking should be the most challenging for ESL students, especially for young adults, who are so self-conscious and so afraid to sound silly and dumb. Speaking requires thinking on one's feet, making spontaneous decisions, exercising independence, and responding to the unexpected in a flexible, creative way. It integrates physical, social, and intellectual forces and undergirds all language skills (Moffett & Wagner, 1992).

The children living in Chinatown have few opportunities to speak English. In school, because of their limited English proficiency, they spend more time on working basic skills worksheets and textbooks than on speaking and doing personally relevant reading and writing. That is why so many ESL Chinese students can barely speak any English after they have been in American schools for two or three years. Speaking is not just one of the language skills, but an essential part of language development and the development of reading and writing skills. Take spelling and vocabulary learning, for example. If we simply let students memorize spelling words, they are not learning to express themselves in a real context; they may pass the spelling test, but they will never have ownership of those words. Only when they can use those words in their speech, will those words become part of their personal vocabulary.

Britton (1972) sees talk as a necessary step to reading and writing: "Talk . . . prepares the environment into which what is taken from reading may be accommodated; and from that amalgam the writing proceeds" (p. 166). Talk helps us make sense of what we read and helps external knowledge become our own. Conversation is an essential step in writing: it helps stimulate our thinking, organize our thoughts, and search for words to catch our fuzzy feelings (Fu, 1995). As ESL teachers, we need to provide as many opportunities as possible for ESL students to speak English, and also understand the stages of their oral language development. Just as children's speech evolves from making random sound, to speaking telegraphic language, to speaking more and more like adults, for these Chinese ESL children, the evolution may progress from speaking mostly Chinese mixed with some English words, to speaking half Chinese and half English, to speaking broken English, until their English becomes more and more standard. If we don't give them chances to speak, then they will never be able to speak, no matter how many years they have been studying in this country. Once I met a 30-year-old Chinese-American man who barely spoke any English. I was shocked to find out that he had been born in this country and had grown up in Chinatown. I can't believe any literacy education program could allow this to happen. Seeing so many students silently practicing their English handwriting and diligently working on worksheets, I am afraid that many of them could turn out to be like that 30-year-old Chinese-American man.

In our educational system, students in honor programs tend to have more opportunity to discuss books and do creative work in reading and writing. ESL students are given little chance to speak and engage in meaningful work, as we tend to think that these students don't have the basic language skills to participate in challenging discussion (Townsend & Fu, 1998). Ironically, what they need the most, we give them the least. Instead of helping them do what they can't do well, we strip any opportunity for them to try, to experiment, to explore a new language territory.

We give less value to oral language at the middle school level because we assume speaking is not as significant as reading and writing, and oral language activities sometimes can seem too childish to middle schoolers. However, when we learn a new language, speaking it can be most rewarding. We tend to get excited when we can make ourselves understood by uttering a few words in a different language. I remember when I first came to this country, how thrilled and proud I was of myself when my utterance in English was accepted by my peers' smiles and nodding of their heads. Their understanding and approval of my English utterance always made me feel I owned those lines and words. To be able to read and write in English didn't give me this same excitement. When I saw how excited the sixth-grade ESL Chinese students were when they presented their puppet shows in this middle school, I understood how they felt about their accomplishment as language learners. Moffett and Wagner (1992) state: "No matter what our age, we never outgrow this need to project feeling into roles we enjoy or need to assume" (p. 97). After presenting their puppet shows, I am sure they not only remember the content of the play, but also feel the ownership of the lines they each spoke and contributed in writing. Isn't this the best way to learn a language, through this integration of reading, writing, and oral language activity?

The key is to make sure that speaking activities are challenging, not childish. If students practice speaking only for the sake of learning language skills, such as memorizing alphabetic letters or language patterns like "this is . . . ," "that is . . . ," "these are . . . ," and "those are . . . ," they will certainly feel they are being treated as less than intelligent. Only when their intelligence has been challenged, their imagination and creativity have been stretched, will they feel that puppet shows, readers' theater, and other oral language activities are worthy of their time. Only when they are able to communicate freely with others will they feel free from being "locked in a cage or cave." The American literacy is the key to unlocking their lonely hearts, to becoming confident enough to find their place in this English-speaking world. They will feel just as I do—that America is their home and that they are on their way to becoming true Chinese-Americans.

References

Britton, J. (1972). *Language and learning.* Harmondsworth, England: Penguin.

Fu, D. (1995). *My trouble is my English: Asian students and the American dream.* Portsmouth, NH: Heinemann.

Krashen, S. (1996). *Under attack: The case against bilingual education.* Culver City, CA: Language Association.

Moffett, J., & Wagner, B. J. (1992). *Student-centered language arts, K–12* (4th ed.). Portsmouth, NH: Heinemann.

Townsend, J., & Fu, D. (in press). "What happened to quiet students?" *English Education.*

Trueba, H., Jacobs, L., & Kirton, E. (1990). *Cultural conflict and adaptation: The case of Hmong children in American society.* New York: Falmer.

6 I Am the Immigrant in My Classroom

Miles Gullingsrud

When I drive the 15 minutes to Westside School each day, I leave the walled country clubs and ritzy neighborhoods of Palm Springs and go down to the massive fields and orchards of the eastern Coachella Valley. My sixth- and seventh-grade "temporary" classroom is shaded by a working grove of towering date palms. The school district office is in Thermal, just up the road from Oasis and Mecca. These gritty communities straddle the railroad tracks and highways leading west to the produce markets of Los Angeles.

In summer, the burning sun blasts every living thing into the ground. In the gorgeous days of winter, people spread out across the land and noisy trains and trucks rumble through loaded with the products of backbreaking labor—grapefruit and garlic, carrots and corn, onions, broccoli, asparagus, and lettuce, and the premiere crops, table grapes and dates.

For 100 miles to the south, the desert marches through moonscape mountains to The Border. Mexico is always just over our horizon.

It has been a long night of parent conferences. The weary man before me wears an old straw cowboy hat and stares at hands he tried to wash. He speaks English with a heavy Spanish accent. "I don't want my kids to grow up to have to work in the fields like me. The work it's hard. Real hard. And not much money. I want better for them."

The message is powerful, but I'm troubled by an air of resignation I've heard in others. The 12-year-old boy between us needs to be strong in ways he doesn't know. He has ability but lacks confidence as a learner. He's not even sure he wants to be a learner. We need to find some worthy goals he can believe in. I'd like to see him excited about school. Is his father going to help in all this?

Reprinted from *Voices from the Middle*, September 1998.

I tell them what I've told many others, that I hope my students learn that all honest labor is honorable, that success begins with learning the right ways from parents, that doing well in school gives them more choices, like finding a job they really want or maybe even college.

Man and boy watch me blankly. I hear myself rattling on. Have I lost them with words they don't understand? Or do they just know better? Do they trust this alien creature across the desk who speaks only English? Do they even like me? Does it matter? Does any of this matter?

Of course it does. This is only November. It's been a long night.

I am the immigrant in my classroom.

When I look at the faces before me, I suppose I feel what it is to be the only foreign student in a class. How can I win acceptance? How can I learn to accept them?

The population of the Coachella Valley Unified School District is 96% "Hispanic," which for us means "Mexican." These people routinely endure the indignities of racial discrimination. A staggering 86% of our population cites Spanish as their first language. If it's their only language, life outside their home community can be difficult. Poverty runs so deep that every child qualifies for free school breakfast and lunch—the government says it's not worth keeping statistics for the few who don't. Our high school dropout and teen pregnancy rates are among the state's highest. Our students fare poorly on state standardized testing.

I marvel to see these kids succeeding in the face of such obstacles. Let it be said, many *do* succeed, thanks to hard work, enthusiasm, support from others, good work habits. I know my middle schoolers arrive in my classroom with such qualities already in place. My job is to find ways to help them grow. I believe my students will teach me these ways if I will only watch and listen. Here's a short list of what we have learned together in 15 years.

1. I work at learning and using Spanish.

Just as we model reading and writing, so our English learners need to see us learning their language as we ask them to learn ours. I don't suppose I'm ever going to become fluent in Spanish, but I *can* be a Spanish learner, showing my students I believe learning a second language is possible and worthwhile.

- I make an effort to use rudimentary expressions such as greetings, common questions, numbers, and days of the week.

- I work on my Spanish accent. I learn to pronounce names correctly before calling roll on opening day.
- I ask for words. I've learned to say, "How do you say _____ in Spanish?" ("¿Cómo se dice _____ en español?")
- I keep translation dictionaries handy for all of us.
- I keep a language learning journal to write down notes and Spanish words or phrases for practicing.
- I read Spanish text to myself and aloud to the kids. I don't understand every thing, but it's the same for my students in English.

I am thrilled when my English learners show me with smiles and words that they appreciate my struggle as I try to use their language.

2. Class lists are created heterogeneously, using a range of language abilities as the criteria.

This makes our English learners full-time members of our school learning community and also gives them successful peer models. (The one obvious exception is the daily period of concentrated "English-as-a-second-language" instruction for English learners.)

3. I cultivate a corps of language brokers.

These are the students I turn to when I have a question about Spanish during discussions, when I'm writing a bilingual note home, or when I need someone to translate for another student. Most are happy to help once I explain how it will assist me and help our English learners succeed in school. The experience is good for their language development as well.

4. I reach out to our English learners to provide an enjoyable school experience.

The longer I teach, the more I value the work of Stephen Krashen and others in affective domain issues. It's easy to focus on instructional practice and forget the importance of helping our English learners feel secure and happy as learners at school. If I don't reach out to give these kids some special attention, they can seem to disappear in a classroom dominated by a language mostly incomprehensible to them.

I look for ways to bond. I find out if their brothers or sisters were students of mine and I ask about their families, because respect for family is paramount in Mexican culture. I go to after-school sports and community events. I display pictures of my family on my desk and share what goes on in my life. I look for things we can smile about.

5. I bring as much primary language text into my room as I can.

Even in my district, where Spanish predominates and bilingual education is a fixture, I'm struck by how little Spanish text has been present until recently, especially in rooms where the teacher speaks no Spanish.

I look for books that I already have in English, or bilingual text within a single volume, so we can all enjoy the same works together. We read aloud side-by-side, one student doing a passage in English and another the same in Spanish. I take part as well, reading either language, and of course I encourage my English learners to try the new language.

There is a growing body of children's fiction in both languages by Chicano authors like Sandra Cisneros and Gary Soto, who also serve as personal models for English learners. Cisneros grew up in a poor neighborhood in Chicago and went to the University of Iowa. Soto was raised in a laboring family in Fresno and became a faculty member at University of California Berkeley. These authors, whose first language was Spanish, draw on their own childhood experiences for topics, making them excellent models for the English learners in my reading and writing workshop setting.

I search bookstores, conference vendors, and catalogs for Spanish text.

6. I do what teachers everywhere do by adapting ideas to the special needs of my class.

"You mean you can actually do workshop with kids like yours?" a colleague asked at a conference, after I told her about my students and how I tried to follow the classroom practices described by Donald Graves, Nancie Atwell, and others like them. My new acquaintance assumed I had no hope of conducting the conferences and minilessons described by those teachers because of the "language barrier."

"Language isn't really a barrier," I told her. "It just makes for rough terrain."

When I come across a grand strategy or simply a short lesson that I like, I tailor it to my students.

My students had a terrific time last year with a unit suggested by the new book *Moon Journals,* which presents a series of writing and art "invitations" based on daily observations of the moon throughout a lunar cycle. Special care was taken to introduce the unit in both languages, in class conversations and in notes to parents. Visual arts, of course, provide avenues of communication free from oral or written language.

7. I learn about my students' culture and give it authentic standing and respect.

I see self-esteem grow in English learners when they find their classmates and I appreciate their culture. They feel comfortable doing familiar activities they might have thought were left behind in Mexico or at home.

We enjoy working with *dichos* (familiar sayings or proverbs), *adivinanzas* (riddles that often involve a play on words), and folktales, all products of a rich folk tradition that can be found in bilingual text settings.

I use several richly illustrated bilingual collections of *dichos.* There are translations of sayings familiar to Americans, like *"El Pájaro que se levanta temprano, agarra primero el gusano* / The early bird gets the worm." There are many uniquely Mexican wisdoms, like *"Entre menos burros, mas olotes* / Among fewer burros, more corncobs."

A favorite folk character is *La Llorona,* the beautiful woman who married above herself and came to drown her children when enraged by her wandering husband. Her mournful spirit is said to be heard crying along waterways and even to appear in ghostly form. I have an engaging bilingual recording of this story by storyteller Joe Hayes of Santa Fe, with an accompanying text in both languages, which never fails to produce a lively class discussion about encounters with the Weeping Woman. Elena once told us straightfaced how her father, driving the family back from Mexicali late one Sunday night, vetoed a roadside potty break by reminding them that *La Llorona* roams the drainage ditches.

Our annual Days of the Dead/*Dias de los Muertos* observance, coincidental with Halloween, has become a "mark your calendar" event, anticipated by students and parents from the first day of school. A cherished tradition throughout Mexico, Days of the Dead commemorates departed family members who are thought to return in spirit to visit the living on All Saints Day.

We write biographical sketches of deceased family members or friends. In prewriting, students interview parents or someone else at home using a bilingual guide. (See Figures 1 and 2.) When these biographies are read aloud by candlelight the night of our "party," it is not unusual to see *mamás y papás* wiping away tears.

We do related art activities such as cast little skulls of hard bread dough and paint them in brilliantly colored motifs. Carlos once represented his favorite professional basketball teams by painting his skulls with the team colors.

We decorate the room, sip traditional hot chocolate, and nibble *pan de muertos* (sweet bread with "bones" baked into the crust), listen to Mexican music, browse through my collection of books that examine the tradition, and watch a commercial video on the subject.

Some Anglos may view the activities of Days of the Dead as gruesome, but Mexicans, while just as prone to grief as anyone, seem more accepting of death as a natural outcome in the process of living, and view this annual event as affirmation of the concept of life after death.

Victor Villaseñor, whose *Rain of Gold* is a powerful history of his family's migration from Mexico to Southern California, is eloquent on the importance of a healthy cultural identity for immigrant children. Talking on CBS's *Sunday Morning* magazine program, he described the trauma of being demeaned by an Anglo teacher. "None of that Mexican stuff," she decreed when she heard Spanish. She even stalked him and his friends to a corner of the playground at recess. "I already told you, none of that Mexican stuff."

Illiterate and bitter, Villaseñor was sent to Mexico for high school to keep him out of trouble. He cried in the interview as he described how overcome he was when he visited the National Museum and viewed the finest artistic representations of his heritage. "I discovered I had a culture," he said.

The late Congressman Sonny Bono said in a local speech several years ago, "English is the only language we should be speaking in America." My students saw the newspaper story and were offended. They wrote their congressman but he did not answer.

I take care not to set up comparisons of cultures that cast one as superior to the other. I'm troubled to hear politicians declare that America "is the greatest country in the world." The implied denigration of all other countries doesn't sit well with me or my students.

Westside School
Monday, October 20, 1997

Dear Parents,

Each of my Language Arts students at Westside School is being asked to write a biography of a family member or friend who has died. I am asking parents or anyone else at home to help with this writing project.

The biography is at the heart of my annual class celebration of the Days of the Dead, the traditional Mexican observance which honors those who have died.

We have celebrated Days of the Dead the past four years as the first special activity of **Tándem**, a program created to bring parents and teachers together with our students for learning and fun.

Each year the celebration gets bigger and better. Save the early evening of Thursday, October 30. Students who volunteer will read their biographies by candlelight. We'll tell you more about our plans soon.

Please help your student write answers to the questions in the attached interview guide which will be used to write the biography. We are interested in things that made the person special to you, things that set them aside, important or unusual things for which they are remembered.

A mother one year thanked me for this assignment with tears in her eyes after hearing her son read about his grandfather, a very lovely man whom the boy had never had a chance to know.

We want our students to learn that we all touch the lives of those around us and that the way we are viewed lives beyond our lifetimes.

Attendance at the evening session is voluntary.

The biography writing is an assignment that will. be graded.

Thank you for joining in this important undertaking,

M.Gullingsrud
M.Gullingsrud

Figure 1. "Days of the Dead" Letter to Parents

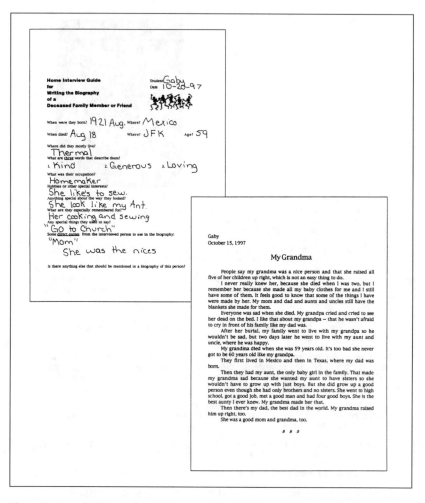

Figure 2. Sample Biography of Deceased Family Member

8. I seek a clear and detailed picture of where each English learner is academically.

It's easy to slip into stereotypical thinking when dealing with a group of people different from you, especially when it's tough to communicate with them. The better I get to know my students as individuals, the better I can manage their learning and the better they respond.

It's crucial to find out as soon as possible how they read in their primary language. There are testing instruments, but I especially value the judgment of a knowledgeable bilingual colleague who has read with the child.

Middle schoolers with limited English proficiency come in many variations. A good number of recent arrivals display a solid command of learning that is obvious despite our language divergence. They exhibit good reading behavior with Spanish text. They are engaged Spanish writers. They do their homework. Their citizenship is exemplary. These kids do everything a teacher could want—they just don't do it in English. They were fortunate to have had schooling in Mexico and have the easiest time moving into English. They bring to mind the adage that we only have to learn to read once.

Other new arrivals aren't so lucky. Formal schooling is not universal in Mexico. If they can't read at all, they need a good bilingual program where they can learn to read in their spoken language and commence content area learning in that language while receiving direct English instruction aimed at eventual fluency. Unfortunately, administrators tend to concentrate scarce Spanish-speaking teachers in the primary grades, where it is thought they stand to do the most good for the greatest number.

I also have students who have been in our bilingual program since Headstart but have not transitioned into English. Some are learning disabled, and I hope that they are being served. Some have not had the benefit of qualified bilingual teachers, which is to say their teachers were just plain ineffective or, more likely, were not Spanish fluent. The California education department says we have never had better than a third of the qualified teachers needed in bilingual programs for English learners, who now comprise about 40 percent of the nation's total.

My district's upper-grade classrooms abound with students who are successful learners thanks to bilingual education, who otherwise would be struggling, if not failing. We also have kids who suffered along the way because too many of their classrooms were not staffed with truly qualified teachers.

Another kind of student presents an unusual circumstance that would not be obvious to a teacher who did not look into individual histories. These children have attended our school for a long time with good bilingual instruction. Nevertheless, they remain Spanish-dependent. The reason is they have no use for English except at school. All their family and neighbors speak Spanish. There is Spanish television, radio, and newspaper. Stores and offices accommodate Spanish. Some of these kids are simply bound to replicate their present existence when they have families of their own.

I do not agonize about their future. I furnish them the opportunity to develop English proficiency and wait for them to make the necessary commitment.

As we help immigrant children acquire the language and learn the ways of a new land, we need to encourage them to maintain respect for their primary language and culture.

Successful middle school teachers know that adolescents, outrageous as they may be at times, deserve to be the age they are—we should not be trying to turn them into pint-sized adults all the time. The same is true for our English learners. They deserve to be proud users of their primary language. They come to it naturally, just as we did to English, and with it comes their culture. That language and that culture command our respect.

It is specifically *not* our job to take them from their place to ours. Rather, we need to help them pack their baggage for a very special journey among the world's many languages and cultures. Their destination is not my world or yours. It is a place of their own making in a future we can only imagine. We need to learn to value and celebrate our differences, which don't amount to much compared to our vast commonalities.

If these children make a good journey, they will come to a place of personal satisfaction in the world as it really is, a world of infinite diversity made by us all.

Selected Resources

Books about Teaching

Atwell, N. (1987). *In the middle: Writing, reading and learning with adolescents.* Portsmouth, NH: Heinemann.

Atwell, N. (1998). *In the middle: New understandings about writing, reading and learning* (2nd ed.). Portsmouth, NH: Heinemann.

Chancer, J., & Rester-Zodrow, G. (1997). *Moon journals: Writing, art and inquiry through focused nature study.* Portsmouth, NH: Heinemann.

Graves, D. (1983). *Writing: Teachers & children at work.* Portsmouth, NH: Heinemann.

Rief, L. (1992). *Seeking diversity: Language arts with adolescents.* Portsmouth, NH: Heinemann.

Books about Teaching English Learners

Freeman, Y. S., & Freeman, D. E. (1992). *Whole language for second language learners.* Portsmouth, NH: Heinemann.

Krashen, S. D. (1985). *Inquiries & insights: Second language teaching, immersion & bilingual education, literacy.* Englewood Cliffs, NJ: Alemany Press.

Rigg, P., & Allen, V. G. (1989). *When they don't all speak English: Integrating the ESL student into the regular classroom.* Urbana, IL: National Council of Teachers of English.

Books about Mexican Culture

Hoobler, D., & Hoobler, T. (1994). *The Mexican-American family album.* New York: Oxford University Press.

Krull, K. (1994). *The other side: How kids live in a California Latino neighborhood.* New York: Lodestar Books.

Sullivan, C. (Ed.). (1994). *Here is my kingdom: Hispanic-American literature and art for young people.* New York: Harry N. Abrams.

Villaseñor, V. (1991). *Rain of gold.* New York: Laurel.

West, J. O. (1988). *Mexican-American folklore: Legends, songs, festivals, proverbs, crafts, tales of saints, of revolutionaries, and more.* Little Rock, AR: August House.

Westridge Young Writers Workshop. (1992). *Kids explore America's Hispanic heritage.* Santa Fe, NM: John Muir.

Books about Days of the Dead

Carmichael, E., & Sayer, C. (1991). *The skeleton at the feast: The day of the dead in Mexico.* Austin, TX: University of Texas Press.

Greenleigh, J. (Photographer). (1991). *The days of the dead: Mexico's festival of communion with the departed.* San Francisco: Collins. [Bilingual]

Hoyt-Goldsmith, D. (1994). *Day of the dead: A Mexican-American celebration.* New York: Holiday House.

Krull, K. (1994). *Maria Molina and the days of the dead.* New York: Macmillan.

Lasky, K. (1994). *Days of the dead.* New York: Hyperion Books for Children.

Literature for English-Learning Children

Alarcón, F. (1997). *Laughing tomatoes and other spring poems/Jitomates risueños y otros poemas de primavera.* San Francisco: Children's Book Press. [Bilingual—English and Spanish in one volume]

Barlow, G., & Stivers, W. N. (1995). *Stories from Mexico/Historias de México.* Chicago: Passport Books. [Bilingual]

Carlson, L. M. (Ed.). (1994). *Cool salsa: Bilingual poems on growing up Latino in the United States.* New York: Henry Holt. [Bilingual]

Cisnernos, S. (1984). *The house on Mango Street.* New York: Vintage Books. [Separate English and Spanish editions available]

Gonzalez, R., & Ruiz, A. (1995). *My first book of proverbs/Mi primer libro de dichos.* Emeryville, CA: Children's Book Press. [Bilingual]

Hayes, J. (1987). *La llorona/The weeping woman.* El Paso, TX: Cinco Puntos Press. [Bilingual Text & Tape Recording]

Lowell, S. (1992). *The three little javelinas.* Flagstaff, AZ: Northland. [English and Spanish]

Paulsen, G. (1993). *Sisters/Hermanas.* New York: Harcourt Brace. [Bilingual]

Paulsen, G. (1995). *The tortilla factory.* New York: Harcourt Brace.

Scieszka, J. (1989). *The true story of the three little pigs.* New York: Viking. [English and Spanish]

Sellers, J. M. (1994). *Proverbios y dichos Mexicanos/ Folk wisdom of Mexico.* San Francisco: Chronicle Books. [Bilingual]

Soto, G. (1985). *Living up the street: Narrative recollections.* New York: Dell.

Soto, G. (1990). *Baseball in April and other stories.* New York: Harcourt Brace. [English and Spanish]

Soto, G. (1991). *Taking sides.* New York: Harcourt Brace.

Soto, G. (1992). *Neighborhood odes.* New York: Harcourt Brace.

Soto, G. (1993). *Too many tamales.* New York: Putnam & Grosset. [English and Spanish]

Catalogues for Mexican Literature & Classroom Products

Ninos, "Your Best Source for Quality Bilingual Products." Genesis Direct, Inc., Customer Care, P.O. Box 1603, Secaucus, NJ 07096-1603. Phone 800-634-3304. FAX 201-583-3644.

Teacher's Discovery, "Complete Sourcebook of Affordable Bilingual Education Supplies." 2741 Paldan Dr., Auburn Hills, MI 48326. Phone 800-TEACHER.

7 Check Out the Real America: Many Hued, Many Tongued, and Many Storied

Anne Fairbrother

My Chicano students taught me how to teach them. I came as a new teacher to my classes in Salinas, California: a white woman, educated in England, profoundly schooled in the canon, a *gringa* who had just started to learn Spanish. And I may have been destined to teach as I was taught, as I have seen many teach since then, if it wasn't that I had taken to heart two tenets from my credentialing course: Build on what the students know and make it relevant to them. So when I saw that most of my students were Chicano, I asked where the Chicano literature was. I was told by my colleagues that there was none—that they would like some, but knew of none.

That started my journey. I read, I explored, I shared books with my fellow teachers. I discovered there *is* a canon of Chicano literature, seminal works from the 1960s and 1970s, inspirations to those who came after. I used the books, the stories, the poems, and I learned from my students as the literature touched their lives, and their lives touched my heart. My journey took me into my community, immersed me in Chicano culture, taught me respect and love as I learned who my students were and the story of the struggles and the triumphs of their history.

It was maybe the most exciting time of my life, an odyssey of learning and enjoyment. And I saw that I owed it to all my students to bring their worlds into the classroom, to echo their voices in the stories we read, to listen to each other's stories and respond to them. I developed and taught an elective in Mexican American literature, a passion for me, but I also offered a variety

Reprinted from *English Journal*, November 1998.

of Chicano texts, along with literature from many other cultures, in my eleventh grade college prep American literature and general tenth grade English classes. I wanted the kaleidoscope that was my class reflected in what we read, what we did, and what we expressed.

At the end of the year, the American literature students explored their own heritage. One student wrote, "To be American means different cultures not just one," and I placed this in the middle of the wall, surrounding it with family trees celebrating many heritages—African, Mexican, European, Asian, Native American—many intertwining of roots, much *mestizaje*. Students wrote poems celebrating who they were, emblazoning the wall with color to match the beautiful diversity in our class.

I learned that we have to ask, Who are our students? What is the world like outside our school doors? How do we help students find out who they are and how they can relate to their community, to the world? This forces us to ask the bigger, harder, but achingly essential question—What is education for? I think part of the answer has to do with allowing literature to touch our students. An African American student may be touched by Richard Wright's painful but relentless journey to identity and also by Gary Soto's feisty growth from childhood. A white student may be touched by the father's anguish as his children grow away from him in *Heart of Aztlán,* and a Chicano who sees his world mirrored in a novel for the first time may write, as did Jorge about *Heart of Aztlán,* "This is the best book I have ever read, in fact it is the only book I have ever read . . ."

To let students make connections is what teaching from multicultural perspectives is about. Most essentially, the connections are within themselves. The one experience that I treasured every year came in that moment when I passed out the short story, the book, the poem, and the quiet Mexican American boy looked and saw Spanish names, the description of a place he knew, of a person who looked like him . . . and then he raised his eyes to me. And I saw hope, I saw a light there, and I read his unspoken question . . . Is it possible? Is my world valid here? And I tell you, if the alienation that causes Latino students to drop out at more than double the rate of white students wasn't too deeply anchored, then that student may have had the first chance to contemplate school success.

To see oneself in the play of things! Before we read Steinbeck's *Of Mice and Men,* we read part of *The Plum Plum Pickers* by Raymond Barrio and part of Carlos Bulosan's autobiography, *America is in the Heart: A Personal History.* The passionate metaphoric descriptions of picking apricots in the blazing sun of the Imperial Valley and the poignant story of the hard journey of a Filipino to the fields of California added to the world of itinerant farm workers that Steinbeck presents in his works. By using such varied texts, the students easily embraced higher thinking skills, seeing connections and understanding commonalities in the respect they developed for difference, for the uniqueness of a cultural heritage. Three Filipina students devoured Bulosan. They had never read anything by a Filipino in their eleven years of schooling, and they wanted more. I gave one girl a novel of Filipino American experience that I had found at a Philippine bookstore in San Francisco. I had a library of Chicano novels and texts that students would borrow from—for book reports in other classes, for research projects, for private reading—and the word spread beyond my classes.

This imperative of the responsibility to honor all our students' lives pervades the curriculum. It means that before we read Huck Finn, I listened to my proud black students who complained that when we talked of black experience, we always started with slavery—as if that was where African Americans started, with a gradual uphill journey from there; as if the white man did eventually save the black man from his fate, his lowly state, because it was for his own good. But if we look back to the cultures from which the men, women, and children were kidnapped to the greatness of the African civilizations, to the wonder that was the fabled Timbuktu, then we find the richness of developed culture and the threads of courage and resistance that have always characterized African American writings. Then we must hear Frederick Douglass's voice beside Jim's; we must show our students that spirit, that strength, that insistence on freedom.

Multicultural education involves decentering whiteness so that cultural relativity may compel what and how we teach. All students benefit from this. I saw white students who relished this rich variety, the colorful and soul-stretching stories. Many students welcomed this glimpse into other cultures, into the life of the student sitting beside them, into the world of a woman a century before, into the life of this continent before the white race claimed it—all told, of course, through the voices of those who know their stories.

I also saw white resistance to this displacing of privilege, and I think this may be the worm in the apple that teachers have to be prepared for as they bring multicultural works into their curriculum as core texts, not as just supplemental works. Young white students may openly complain and arrogantly ask when we will be getting back to the real literature. White culture and concerns and the Eurocentric telling of history have become the norm, and those young students well know that outside my classroom the dominant culture is still alive and dominating, and that the icons of white experience and achievement still inform all expressions of culture, power, and privilege. They know that and understandably expect school to continue to validate their world. This may be the biggest challenge for teachers, and one they have to deal with.

I dealt with this challenge early in the school year by raising the comfort level with diversity, by validating all cultural perspectives through student responses to the moving fifteen-minute section on California Indians from the video series *500 Nations,* which showed the Chumash experience at the hands of the Spanish missionaries, the newly independent Mexicans, and the gold-seeking Americans. From the students' reactions to the continuum of responses that emerged, it was clear that permission to explore all perspectives became unthreatening and enjoyable. Positions could be relaxed, prejudices abandoned. Certainly the *issue* of multiple perspectives needs to be addressed to diffuse resistance and hostility, to allow the kaleidoscope full expression.

I work with preservice teachers now, fledglings trying out their teacher wings for the first time. As the teaching profession becomes increasingly white and the student population increasingly diverse, it is imperative that we help student teachers understand who their students are and learn to teach in ways and with materials that are different from the familiar. I find some student teachers hungry for new materials, eager to embrace their students' worlds, committed to extending their students' horizons. Some student teachers easily grasp ideas of how white hegemony pervades the curriculum and the school culture, and some will pioneer change. A young man whose final project was an impressive unit of African American poetry tells me of what he has to teach in his upcoming student teaching placement—a classic example of texts written by dead white males. When he asked his female cooperating teacher why there were no women's voices, no diversity of cultural perspectives, she told him that these canonized texts were the works that students needed to read, presumably the important components of cultural literacy that constitute the default setting of schooling in America.

There is a long way to go, but we have to be able to answer student teachers' questions about meeting the needs of students and handling the diversity of today's classrooms. The evidence is right under our noses as we meet daily with our students. What is the percentage of minority students in

AP classes? What is the percentage of minority students in remedial English classes? I can predict that the first percentage will be a lot smaller than the second. And why is this? If we don't accept the racist idea that darker skin color correlates with lower intelligence, then we have to look for the reason in the process of education itself, in the institution of education itself. We have to ask why the dropout rate for Chicano, Native American, and African American students is so much higher than that of Anglo and Asian students. We have to look at the educational experience of the captured, conquered, and colonized—in the past and in the present in America. We have to look at how the culture of our educational system is socializing students and at the alienation experienced by those students who do not see themselves as Anglo. We must include all students in an education that socializes them to a multicultural rather than a monocultural America.

Indeed, this principle necessitates that we also allow our white students to rediscover their stories, because they are too often denied the knowledge of the spectrum of their heritage. When my students indicated on their family trees, their maps of heritage, where their families came from, it was the white students who often said "American," starting and ending their cultural identity there. "But," I said to them, "unless you are American Indian or *mestizo,* your family came from somewhere, probably somewhere in Europe. Where was that?" They asked their parents and sometimes discovered a path into the past, but many times nothing was known. Failure to pass on family stories was often a conscious choice of immigrants—sadly, sometimes from coercion—in their desire to be American. Indeed, assimilation, the key to future success, required such a sacrifice of the past. So we must acknowledge the diversity of European Americans, whose great-grandchildren sit in our classrooms, and we must further enhance the literary kaleidoscope with, for example, Jewish American, Italian American, Anglo American, and Irish American stories and experiences. It is imperative that *all* students see themselves and each other as part of the kaleidoscope of the classroom, of society, so they can explore what it is to be American.

As my students' poems show, there is joy in acknowledged, validated, celebrated diversity, and there is wonder and anguish in the tentative exploration of self as students seek identity. We as English teachers should bring that joy and that exploration to our classrooms in the literature we read, the stories we elicit, the questions we pose and answer. We don't teach English, we teach students. My students taught me well. ¡Qué viva el caleidoscopio!

What Am I?

I am Filipino American
Kamusta! Hello!

I am born in America, but my parents were not.
Everyone is like family.

Anyone older than me can be my aunt or uncle.
I have the best of both worlds.

Tagalog the language most spoken, I understand some.
We are found to be short . . . but does that matter?

Lumpia is usually around the house to eat.
Halo-Halo is my favorite dessert treat.

I am proud of my ethnic culture
I am who I am forever there is no other.

Filipino American.

                                    —Elaine Flores

African Americans

Dark, tall, beautiful people.
We walk the earth just like everyone else.
People look at us in weird ways.
And some call us names because of our color.
We were brought here as slaves.
And treated like dirt and trash.
They call us Negroes and colored
Because of what we looked like on the outside
Some wonder why?
What did we do to cause so much hatred.
My people in Africa is strong and beautiful.
There is many a thing that we have made
And did not receive credit for nor respect.
I wish I knew how to speak the
language of my people.
Even the tribes that carried
throughout the African life.
Someday we are going to rise up.
There have been many ancestors who

are memorable and have made a positive
contribution to our people.
We are getting some of our
respect and joy back after all
these long years.

—Yashame Tell

One Nation

Redman, Yellowman, Whiteman, & Blackman,
You are all my people,
All two legged hoppers working on Earth,
Moving in all directions,
Ending up at the other person's space,
"Welcome" (Mi casa Su casa)
Kind, generous, caring, loving, respecting, sharing,
One another
Learning to live together in Harmony,
Just as Earth lives with us,
Each direction, color, race, religion
Making up that sacred circle.
Together on Earth
ONE NATION

—Jaime Lemus

Mirror into the Past

I look into the mirror and see the reflections
of relatives long ago.
Some still living, and some dead, who I'll never know.
Azteca blood running through Spanish veins.
My mother's heart and my father's name.

—Pedra Mendoza Jr.

The Beauty of Myself

Who's to say what I am,
some of this and some of that,
I usually say I am just black,
that answer never seems to be good enough,

people always say you don't look just black,
they always say you have to be more than that.
Why should it matter what I am,
I am me and that is that.

—La Shaunda Coleman

The Beauty of Two Cultures

I'm a part of two cultures different in ways
Both are beautiful and strong
It makes me feel pride and honor for my people
One brought us jazz, hip-hop and rap
The other brought us Mozart
One brought us strong leaders such as
Nelson Mandela, Martin Luther King Jr., and Malcolm X.
Leaders who instilled fighting for rights and bravery.
The beauty of my two cultures are combined in me
Both make me more knowledgeable and have a variety
    of ideas
It's the difference in ways which makes me grateful
I'm a part of two cultures.

—Renee McFarland

This is Me:
25% Japanese,
but yet, 100% American,
Blonde hair,
going brown,
Rosy cheeks
on pale white skin,
A foreign tongue,
speaking English,
wearing blue jeans,
The moon, The sun,
Just as ONE.

—Brandi Morris

I am American and proud to be.
The diversity in my cultures is what makes me different;
unique.
With German, Indian, and Japanese blood flowing through

my heart and soul,
My heritage is my foundation, my cultures make me whole.
I am proud of who I am, and I take great pride in my
country,
Great cultures such as mine flood America from sea to
beautifully shining sea.

—Shauna Lee Simpson

8 Language, Literature, and Learning in the ESL Classroom

Mary Kooy and Annette Chiu

Increasingly complex and diverse cultures challenge ESL[1] teachers to find ways of teaching English that stimulate students and ultimately get the job done—as quickly as possible. What are English teachers to do? Frequently, they choose from a selection of English exercises and abridged books that detail how English works but don't necessarily produce language proficiency. Annette's story of her Hong Kong English teaching experience can help us tease out ways of learning English where language and cultural landscapes are shaped simultaneously through engaging students in the growing body of multicultural literature. We ask, with a nod to Tina Turner, "What's literature got to do with it?" As it turns out—plenty.

Annette's Story: English Teaching in Hong Kong

Two years ago, standing before twenty students in my English literature class, *Romeo and Juliet* in hand, an overwhelming feeling of doubt suddenly swept over me: Of what relevance could Shakespeare possibly be to twenty Hong Kong Chinese girls, some of whom could barely cope with their limited English language facility? How could I share my passion for literature with these students if I myself doubted the text's ability to draw them in? To complicate matters, the Hong Kong education system mandates that a teacher's primary—and sometimes sole—responsibility is to make sure her students pass the public exams. Teachers make educated guesses at what

---

Reprinted from *English Journal*, November 1998.

that year's exam questions might be by checking previous exams and intentionally teaching toward them.[2] Classroom content not directly connected to the exams merits open disapproval from school administrators, parents, and often the students themselves.

During the course of the year, I struggled to balance teaching the requirements with what I perceived to be relevant to these adolescents. For instance, though I required memorizing the handbook definitions of literary terms, I also focused on such issues as the generation gap and the resulting attitudes toward love and marriage—both being "hot" items of discussion in the media at the time. In the context of a traditional, conservative society, the Hong Kong students found much to say when I drew in comparisons to North American attitudes.

Somehow, though, things did not seem to balance. I remained frustrated at what I perceived were missing dimensions of a literature class. Certainly the students engaged in dialogue inspired by the text, but because not one of the course's texts[3] reflected the lives of contemporary Hong Kong youth, I felt my students were unable to position themselves meaningfully in the world of the text or in relation to the literary characters. I felt that even though they were responding to questions I designed, the framework was imposed. Because they were alienated by the text, they would always be engaging from a disadvantaged position. I understood the argument that Shakespeare expounded "universal values," and identification with characters could be inspired by elements other than the obvious similarities of time, experience, or geography. Nevertheless, my concern for identification with characters and situations to evoke strong responses in readers remained; the prescribed texts could not resonate sufficiently with my students. Perhaps I'd feel differently if I counterbalanced Shakespeare with a Hong Kong author, and my students could be the "experts" on some aspect of the text, such as the cultural context. Although the year was rich with new teaching experiences, I found it frustrating to leave with many questions about teaching English literature to students whose first language is not English.

Mary's View: A Story of Re-Vision

I teach in a preservice teacher education program, where Annette was a student in my English methods class during the 1996–97 school year. Currently, Annette teaches in a secondary English department. I am a Dutch Canadian immigrant, and Annette is a first generation Chinese Canadian. We have both struggled with issues of culture and language. As a result, we found the Hong Kong narrative and experience a salient starting point for reviewing our thinking about ESL teaching and learning. It provided both pause and opportunity to examine the framework and goals of literature teaching in ESL contexts. Questions emerged: Why the tensions between the two models of English education? How do we structure a secure basis for selecting texts and creating strategies for engaging students of diverse cultures with literature?

The pressure for Annette to focus on measurable language skills in Hong Kong typifies the "disproportionate emphasis on the structure of language" (Sauvé 19) in much ESL teaching. Reading comprehension skills, grammar, and vocabulary exercises—of little immediate relevance or importance to students—constitute the core of ESL curriculum and practices. The focus on skills is interpreted as foundational to learning language.

But language study as an end in itself rarely meets expectations. For Annette, it led to frustration that she was teaching her Hong Kong students "how to speak, read and write in English in a learning situation in which there is little of substance worth talking about" (Handscombe 334). Yet teachers tend to delay challenging ESL students with substantive language experiences until they are judged competent in basic English language skills. The problem is, of course, that language is too complex and does not readily yield to "how to" instructions or a linear process.

A preoccupation with language skills assumes that our language-rich students (many of whom already speak two or more other languages) will develop proficiency through the often random "spattering" of language exercises. We urge a broader vision: language by downpour or immersion. Literature—a place where language and meaning meet—offers a significant source. Povey suggests:

> Literature gives evidence of the widest variety of syntax, the richest variations of vocabulary discrimination. It provides examples of the language employed at its most effective, subtle, and suggestive. As literature sets out the potential of the English language it serves as an encouragement, guide, target to the presently limited linguistic achievement of the foreign student. (162)

Literature, then, merits its own place in ESL teaching and learning—not only for its intrinsic worth, but as an integral part of a language-learning program.

Literature as Cultural "Voices"

Traditionally, ESL classes serve as the entry point for new immigrants to gain language proficiency and a cultural perspective and simultaneously establish a place for themselves within their new environments. Since assimilation to the English speaking environment and culture is often a primary goal, ESL teachers select Western European and North American literature to represent North American culture. An extreme example of assimilation occurred in Canada with the "residential school" experiment where native children were taken from the reservations and placed in often faraway schools to rid them of their language and culture to transform thinking, acting, talking, and worshiping into the likeness of the dominant white culture. Is acculturation and assimilation the task of the ESL class? Exactly what are American and Canadian cultures?

Social and cultural contexts in the United States and Canada have shifted dramatically, particularly in the last generation. A United Nations report has again declared Toronto the world's most multicultural city. When Mary landed in Canada in the 1950s, her peers saw her as "other." They had never encountered her language, clothing, or food. Today, in some urban schools, fifty to sixty different languages can be heard in the hallways. In some, a majority of students speak English as their second language. Social contexts continue to change and with them the need to redefine who we are and what we include in our operating cultural definitions. In this complex, ever-shifting context, ESL teachers can create classes where students become "one of us" without necessarily becoming "like us" and, in the process, form an inclusive cultural community.

As new residents continue to populate our classes, ESL teachers struggle with the realities of students who need to learn the language quickly and be included in school cultures and classes. We propose making a grand turnabout in traditional ESL teaching: Begin with literature and, from the literary experiences, move into and incorporate language study. Unlike "language pullout," where the exercise becomes the focus, beginning with literary texts as contained units with a beginning, middle, and end makes sense. Such texts meaningfully trace the worlds, events, lives, and experiences of others.

How can students who have little knowledge of English begin with literature? If we use a tapestry metaphor, current practice recommends focusing on the individual threads, neglecting the "big picture." Instead, teachers should discern the overall patterns of the work and move toward examining individual textures and threads. This means finding texts that are, even at the beginning stages, accessible and challenging, depicting a wide variety of topics, issues, and just plain good stories.

So we argue for ESL curricula and practices that begin with meaning through immersion in literature. What follows describes how we began to make sense of Annette's Hong Kong experience.

Selecting Literature: Constructing Literary Landscapes

Like Annette in Hong Kong, ESL teachers commonly relate difficulties in choosing appropriate and accessible texts. Commonly available abridged versions or reductions with adjusted vocabulary or length, though they seem to offer easy solutions, dehydrate the essence of literature, its language. Too often, these versions become the vehicles for teacher-produced skill exercises and vocabulary studies. Complete texts, on the other hand, challenge students in their original form by telling the whole story and using original, authentic vocabulary not contrived to mask as grammar or usage lessons.

Because ESL classes often serve as a cultural introduction, decisions on which texts can be labeled American or Canadian are borne by ESL teachers. Since most books available in our book rooms fall under the "traditional canon" category, we continue to bring other texts that engage students into the ESL class. This may be particularly true for texts reflecting a multicultural presence (as San Francisco's recent move to "balance the canon" attempts to do). When students recognize and bring their own experience to a text, the focus shifts away from a lack of English language proficiency (deficit) to knowledgeable individuals with unique ancestries and experiences (Ende and Kocmarek 115).

Literature as a primary source for acculturation, even unconsciously, presents some pitfalls—stereotypes, for instance, that mask or simplistically characterize a culture. The often blurred boundaries between a teacher's obligation to direct students to a particular understanding of the context of the work and the tendency to thereby limit students' understanding, reflects a teacher's living reality. *Anne of Green Gables,* though considered a traditional representation of Canadian experience, does not allow us to use Anne as a model young Canadian. In Hong Kong, for instance, students who read Anne's story generated numerous assumptions about Annette's life as a young Canadian woman—few of them accurate. Recently, Frank McCourt's *Angela's Ashes,* a memoir of his childhood in Ireland, caused quite a stir in his homeland. "That's not us," Irish people said. "Not all Irish are poor nor are all Irish men drunks." That is undoubtedly true.

Our aim in acculturating new residents reflects an inclusive sampling of all that North American literature has to offer. No one text or student can be expected to represent a full picture of any culture or people. It's not that any one representation—limited as it may be—is necessarily bad in and of itself. (McCourt's book is a moving testimony to that fact.) Rather, each text offers a glimpse, and the more glimpses we offer, the bigger and richer the picture becomes.

We recognize the pitfalls of literature charged with the responsibility of "acculturation" yet need to ensure that voices and faces of new residents are included. When we engage students in the works of North Americans such as Louise Erdrich and Thomas King (aboriginal), Toni Morrison (African American), Rohinton Mistry (East Indian), and Choi Kyong-do (Korean), for instance, we participate in extending and (re)shaping our understandings of "culture." After all, these authors live and write here; each one "represents" our culture, and in our readings of their texts, we shape understanding of and participation in a shared cultural context.

The epigraph introducing the one-act play, "Toronto at Dreamer's Rock" by native Canadian playwright Drew Hayden Taylor, reads:

> Stories are memories
> that must be shared with the Universe
> because if they aren't
> the Universe becomes a much smaller place.

Taylor's words can guide our reading selections. If North America's cultural fabric is an ever-growing and changing tapestry, then each story, each cultural representation is another thread, an integral piece of the design. At the same time, teachers can welcome the cultural and individual perspectives students bring to further fortify the reading experience.

Texts of varied language complexities and cultural representations replace stereotypical offerings ("easy" versions of the classics, for instance). A variety of textual forms, writers, topics, and perspectives explores and expands language possibilities for reading and learning. Picture books, often neglected in teaching adolescents, offer accessible and powerful entries into whole texts supported by visual representations as varied as the texts themselves. Some are created for adults; many tackle varied and challenging issues. The narratives in books by writers such as Chris Van Allsburg can be complex and compelling and exhibit art worthy of gallery display. Following are some examples of literature that may expand student perspectives.

Picture Books

The rationale for the common practice of acculturating immigrants through works in the canon can be traced back to the mistaken belief that Columbus discovered a new world rather than stumbled upon peoples with established cultures that rivaled or surpassed those of their European visitors. The picture book *Encounter* by Jane Yolen, illustrated by David Shannon, tells the Columbus story through the eyes of a young native boy who is present but silent during "contact." For those with limited English proficiency, the book, and many others like it, provides a catalyst for discussion of authentic and pertinent issues using striking visuals to support the written text. Students not only gain new vocabulary, they also use the vocabulary to engage in literary discussions (the language of and in literature).

Drama

"Education is our Right," from *Two One-Act Plays* by Drew Hayden Taylor, reinvents the ghosts of Education Past, Present, and Future borrowed from Dickens' *A Christmas Carol* to show how the Minister of Indian Affairs (a government position traditionally known for its patronizing attitudes toward native peoples) has erred. Discussion might include concepts of marginalization (such as the native peoples in their own lands). The counterbalance that a local Hong Kong author would have been to Shakespeare in Annette's Hong Kong classes is similar to the effect of Taylor's take on Dickens' work. We propose that, instead of rewriting the canon, we include a range of texts to inform and enrich the discussion and cultural understanding.

Short Stories

Tales from Firozsha Baag, a collection of short stories by Rohinton Mistry, a Canadian author of East Indian ancestry, are readily accessible to ESL students and offer topics for rich discussion. Set in India, the stories offer glimpses into the lives of Bombay apartment tenants. The characters—at the same time quirky and not particularly unusual—portray very real people. Hindi expressions scattered freely throughout the text offer students a chance to guess the meanings from the context, a viable and helpful language activity.

Novel

Gloria Naylor's *The Women of Brewster Place* weaves the tales of seven individual African American women as they struggle to survive through interdependence and self-identification, important issues for all adolescents.

Poetry

"The Immigrants" by Margaret Atwood captures the alienation and despair of newcomers as they see their dreams for their new home unrealized and destroyed. Though having a common theme, this poem includes the voice of a long-time resident ("I"). As the immigrants see their dreams fade, the "I" in the poem says, "I wish I could forget them / and so forget myself," perhaps highlighting the mutual challenges to the ever-shifting cultural landscape for all who live there.

Reading and Reflecting: The Language "Think Pad"

The questions remaining for Annette as she left her students in Hong Kong could be met in part by revising her text selections, but selection alone does not tell the whole story. How can we meaningfully and actively engage ESL students in texts with an eye to improving their language and literary skills and experiences?

Texts alone do not change ESL classes or mystically improve language. How the texts are read and shared brings language to life and life to the literature. Reading aloud, for instance, a practice generally abandoned after elementary school, gives students new to English an opportunity to hear the language and begin to imagine the narrative. As for young children, read-aloud books can stretch beyond listeners' personal reading comprehension capabilities; they need not understand every word to benefit, though good reading aloud makes a difference. Books with powerful language and perhaps visual support ease the process for newcomers. They can follow along as the reading occurs to both hear and see the text. But students also need ample reading experience daily—alone or with a partner. Texts of all kinds, ranging from picture books to poetry, can fill the shelves and find their way onto tables and into backpacks. Reading improves reading.

Sharing a class text—often a challenging task given the range of language proficiency in any given ESL class—draws together a community in a shared experience and calls on those proficient in English to support others around them. Issues arising out of shared texts can give readers the language for speaking to those issues. Annette's "hot" topics provided her students with motivation to talk. They needed to find the language to make it happen.

Book clubs, so popularized by Oprah Winfrey, can also get students reading and sharing their reading with others. Selecting from five or six titles and book summaries, students can sign up for a preferred text and, with others, begin to read, discuss, write, and represent their thinking. Language immersion becomes central to these ways of reading.

Many students new to English, aware of their limited English proficiency, are reluctant to risk speaking out in class. A study conducted by a colleague revealed that Chinese students resist speaking English in school because their peers interpret it as a way of "showing off" (Goldstein 363). Yet we know that, like most skills, language develops and improves through overt and extensive use.

One way to overcome and meet these challenges is to provide a place for students to articulate their thinking in reading logs ("think pads"). As students read or listen to texts, they regularly stop to "pause and think" by sketching, diagraming, listing (un)familiar words, asking questions, or stating a fact about a character or event. For ESL students, this offers two distinct advantages: (1) the active use of language to think about and understand the world of the texts, and (2) the acknowledgment of their world experiences to interpret and understand texts (Kooy and Wells 115). As readings progress, logs become a scrapbook of learning, a concrete record of their ongoing journeys through and with texts.

Why is writing/representing about thinking so important to this process? First, every reader participates—not only those prepared to respond orally—in literary conversations. Moreover, readers who record their thoughts in logs, as Tammy, a high school sophomore said, "have to concentrate more. And because you're concentrating, you're learning. Because there's no way you could write anything down if you weren't concentrating!" Recording their thinking also gives ESL students "rehearsal" time before any discussions take place as well as a literary vocabulary that admits them to literary discussions and communities—incredibly important to newcomers to English.

As our students read and respond to texts together, we rotate around the room to provide support, get a sense of their reactions, or call for suggestions gleaned from their logs. We regularly collect the logs where we "talk" with each reader in the margins—asking questions, making suggestions, expressing surprise at a new way of understanding a ritual or concept, explaining an unfamiliar word. In the process, we engage in dialogue with readers and come to know them in new ways. As research has shown, the reading log provides evidence of student thinking, a "window" into the reader's mind.

Teachers sometimes tell me that log writing becomes tedious; their students resist. We found that this most often happens when log entries do not lead directly to some accounting of the response either orally or in exchanges with peers or teachers. Logs are intended not only to get the reading process started but to provide opportunities for bringing students' thoughts, predictions, guesses, or questions forward. Students are motivated to stay on task when they are responsible and accountable for their thinking and will be expected to speak from and to the topic journalized. They realize and expect that the writing will be acted upon. The log accompanies the students throughout their reading experiences; it becomes their travel log.

Talking about the Texts Together

Reluctance to speak out in class is not limited to native speakers of English. Nonnative speakers find the risk of speaking up even more daunting. Reading logs become "texts for talk"—discussion prompts for interactions with peers. Particularly for ESL students, formulating ideas and the language to express them in a log before committing to discussion gives them precious time to think and use language, to find something to say.

The interactions during discussions spark new thinking, questions, and discoveries. As in most learning situations, the language is often tentative, uncertain. In discussions, students actively use and hear the language. If discussions begin in small groups, students have an additional occasion to rehearse their language in less intimidating situations and, in the process, prepare for whole class discussion. These represent active learning rehearsals crucial to developing language skills.

Talking about literature with others has other benefits. Readers in a class get to know other readers—their insights, visions, questions, and views of the world. The focus moves away from language deficiencies to knowledge to be shared. As mentioned earlier, Annette found discussions became highly animated and informed when she introduced "hot" issues arising out of the readings, such as the different attitudes held by older and younger generations toward love and marriage. Students articulated differences in traditions, values, and expectations and compared them to the literature and Annette's stories of her North American experiences. A need and desire to express and participate prompted their dynamic participation.

Recently, one of Mary's student teachers taught a short story involving an arranged marriage. He read the story aloud and as a homework assignment asked students to prepare a paragraph describing how they would feel if their parents selected their lifetime partner. As the class filed out, one girl lingered. "Sir," she said, "Did you know that Sunitha's engaged to be married to a guy chosen by her parents? How will she do this assignment?" The student teacher had never considered this possibility. He was flummoxed. How do we change this into a learning situation? What kind of classroom atmosphere must exist to allow Sunitha a place to speak to the issue? Her experiences could contribute valuable insights to the discussion and not only affect the thinking of her peers, but in the process of thinking and speaking clarify her own understanding as well. When our discussions encourage and include many threads of experience, we see the world of the text in new ways. We add texture to our readings.

Interactive discussions establish, link, and maintain an active community of readers that fosters membership into the literary community. Student reflections both in the logs and in their talk make a difference in how they and their peers construct understanding and make sense of texts and, in the process, give them a language for talking about texts. Optimum learning takes place when seamless transitions and interdependence among writing, talking, and reading occur naturally in literature experiences.

Conclusion

As we reflect on teaching experience with ESL students, we find that our conceptions and ideas have changed: "What relevance does Shakespeare have in the lives of Hong Kong girls?" has been answered partially by our own (re)negotiations of what "relevance" means. First, we would amend the syllabus for our English classes to include works in English by a range of authors who bring distinct and diverse visions of what it means to be American or Canadian. Next, we have come to recognize the importance of the literature teacher as facilitator. We cannot rely on the qualities of a text alone to engage the reader. The strategies used to pique student interest and prompt discussion are key to making literature an integral part of the English learning process. Students deeply involved in literature simultaneously acquire the English language and shape their cultural understandings.

Notes

1. In using the term ESL, we also include English as a Foreign Language (EFL) and English Skills Development (ESD).

2. In fact, it is a common practice for teachers not only to teach the answers to anticipated questions, but often to give "model answers," which results in many students memorizing these model answers and regurgitating them at the exams. There are many other issues involved that make the teaching of English in Hong Kong a very complex and highly political exercise—for example, the colonial legacy—but they are stories for another time.

3. Texts are determined by the Examination Authority, based on the British "O" and "A" level syllabi, but selections are antiquated in that all authors are traditional white European, American, or Australian.

Works Cited

Atwood, Margaret. "The Immigrants." *Breaking Through: A Canadian Literary Mosaic.* Ed. John Borovilos. Scarborough, ON: Prentice-Hall, 1990.

Ende, Cheryl, and Ivan Kocmarek. "Using Literature in the ESL Classroom." TESL 90: Reading into the Future—Proceedings of the 1990 TESL Ontario Conference. Eds. J. Sivell and L. Curtis. 114–124.

Goldstein, Tara. "Bilingual Life in a Multilingual High School Classroom: Teaching and Learning in Cantonese and English." *The Canadian Modern Language Review* 53.2 (1997): 356–372.

Handscombe, Jean. "Putting It All Together." *Educating Second Language Children: The Whole Child, The Whole Curriculum, The Whole Community.* Ed. Fred Genesee. New York: Cambridge University Press, 1994. 331–356.

Kooy, Mary, and Jan Wells. *Reading Response Logs: Inviting Students to Explore Novels, Short Stories, Plays, Poetry, and More.* Portsmouth, NH: Heinemann, 1996.

McCourt, Frank. *Angela's Ashes.* New York: Scribner, 1996.

Mistry, Rohinton. *Tales from Firozsha Baag.* Toronto, ON: Penguin Canada, 1991.

Montgomery, L. M. *Anne of Green Gables.* New York: Grosset & Dunlap, 1935.

Naylor, Gloria. *The Women of Brewster Place.* New York: Penguin, 1983.

Povey, John. "The Teaching of Literature in Advanced ESL Classes." *Teaching English as a Second or Foreign Language.* Eds. Marianne Celce-Murcia and Lois McIntosh. Rowley, MA: Newbury House Publishers, Inc., 1979. 162–186.

Sauvé, Virginia. "Working with the Cultures of Canada in the ESL Classroom: A Response to Robert Courchêne." *TESL Canada Journal* 13.2 (1996): 17–23.

Taylor, Drew Hayden. *"Toronto at Dreamer's Rock", and "Education Is Our Right": Two One-Act Plays.* Saskatoon, SA: Fifth House Publishing, 1990.

Yolen, Jane. *Encounter.* New York: Harcourt Brace, 1992.

III How Politics Have Shaped Our Thinking and Our Classrooms

Preservice teachers often enter the field unaware of political influences on the decisions they make about their teaching. As awareness develops, many cry out that they do not care about politics, they simply want to be left alone to teach their students. Unfortunately, such isolation was never possible. Education has always been a political arena, and teaching has always been a highly political act. Instruction and politics share a dialectical relationship: each is influenced by the other.

      Sheridan Blau's inaugural address provides specific illustrations of the current political climate and its influence on educational attitude and practice. He describes conflicts of interest and special interest gain resulting from narrow prescriptions of how teachers should teach the English language arts. With this in mind, Diane Stephens and Nancy Goulden explain the importance of teachers having access to a broad range of information so that they can make professional decisions on what and how to implement in their classrooms with full awareness of competing ideologies. Finally, Roberta Herter describes negotiations that must occur as politically conscious teachers integrate a progressive agenda into a language arts classroom.

9 Toward the Separation of School and State

Sheridan Blau

Like many English teachers of my generation—a generation that graduated from college after the intellectual and ethical atrocities of the McCarthy era but before the Peace Corps and the anti-war marches on Chicago and Washington—I don't like to talk much about politics. Aside from what I believe to be a healthy distrust and distaste for political discourse, I find events on the political scene trivial compared to the consequential matters that are at issue in moral discourse or the discourse of literature. Literature, Ezra Pound insisted—Ezra Pound, who was wise about literature but foolish about politics—"Literature," he said, "is news that stays news" (1960, p. 29). Political goings on are news but, unlike literature, news is fittingly reported in the daily newspaper and just as fittingly discarded with the daily trash. The discourse of politics is no more likely to offer us wisdom for life than the discourse of the popular or the fashionable. For political opinion, like public opinion in general, is often fickle, subject to manipulation by the media, or else designed to *do* the manipulating, and frequently—always in the case of mobs and groups of extreme partisans—not subject to governance by reason, rules of consistency, or reflection.

The Current Scene in the Politics of Education

Those of us who teach in the field of English and the language arts have lately seen our subject and our teaching enter the discourse of politics and become the topic for popular discussions about the "crisis" in public

Reprinted from *Language Arts*, February 1998.

education,[1] so much so that we find ourselves caught in a tide of public opinion that is rising against much of what we stand for intellectually and professionally. Nor is there any shortage of politicians with fingers poised on the public pulse, ready to turn popular prejudice into public policy, especially if they can do so in the name of reliable, replicable, scientific research. Such challenges require us to abandon our diffidence and, however reluctantly, address the political issues.

In state houses, in local school boards, and in Congress, legislators and other policy makers are busy trying to rescue American education by mandating how children should be taught reading, what bodies of research should inform teaching practice in the teaching of reading, and who should be allowed to educate reading teachers and prospective teachers. California has adopted legislation (already successfully copied in the House of Representatives) that would fund inservice programs only when the providers of inservice pass tests, not of their academic credentials but of their subscription to certain acceptable theories of learning, research findings, and instructional practices, forsaking all alternative theories, bodies of research, and unapproved practitioners of research and instruction.

Such legislation serves not merely to privilege particular versions of science and scientific truth over others, but to suppress or disenfranchise alternative accounts of what is true and to discount entirely all research or evidence that derives from research methodologies that do not fit a reductivist, positivist, quantifiable, behaviorist version of scientific research. In the name of education and science, policy makers and a few of their scientific cronies[2] are conducting a campaign for intellectual control and the repression of alternative views that not only threatens the principle of academic freedom but stands opposed to the true aims of science and education. Intellectual suppression can produce only false knowledge (a knowledge that prevents further learning) and a science that substitutes the idolatry of orthodox belief and political expediency for fidelity to the disinterested advancement of learning.

If political history and the history of ideas in the western literary and religious traditions teach us anything, it is to distrust those who not only claim to own the exclusive truth but who insist further on suppressing or punishing all messengers of alternative versions of truth. One of the surest signs of false science has always been its attempt to suppress the arguments and research of those who would challenge its conclusions. Another has been its alignment with sources of political power from which the suppression of alternative ideas always flows. Think of the political figures and governments of the past that have embraced one group of scientists to the exclusion of all others and you will have a catalogue of demagogues and shameful public policies that have used science to justify slavery, racism, genocide, the incarceration of dissidents in mental hospitals, and a host of other injustices.

But let us not overstate the case. Can government agencies and policy makers really be accused of suppressing ethnographic research, case-study research, and most teacher-research—virtually all qualitative research—merely by deciding that the only fundable inservice programs are those based on quantitative, behaviorist research (which is what the California legislature has done and the House of Representatives has approved in House Resolution H.R. 2614)? Only if the prejudice of government policy makers translates into diminished opportunities for certain researchers and research-based programs to find support and obtain a hearing within the educational community. And that, of course, is precisely what is happening, quite aside from the diminished opportunities that are legislatively mandated for politically unacceptable researchers and curriculum specialists. With stories that remind us eerily of the red-baiting days of the '50s we now hear regularly of incidents like the one recently reported on e-mail networks about a small, central California town in which the superintendent of schools canceled a scheduled presentation by a leading language arts researcher (whose publications are widely respected) merely because a couple of teachers complained that she was "too whole language." The superintendent claimed that he didn't know anything about the speaker he had canceled, but the accusation about her professional affiliation was enough for him to withdraw an invitation, to break a contract, to suppress the dissemination of findings from a professionally respectable line of research.

The Professional Debate vs. The Political Debate

Let us be clear about what we stand for and what we oppose. As a profession, and as members of a professional organization we are not combatants—despite the desire of journalists—in any war between the proponents of a whole language approach to literacy and a phonics-based approach. Researchers and practitioners who are experts (as I am not) from both sides of this artificial divide demonstrate in most of their writing and presentations that they represent different emphases and different research traditions in a field that can accommodate and benefit from a variety of research perspectives and a rich variety of instructional approaches.

Responsible researchers and teachers who tend to favor either school of thought regularly employ methods and findings identified with the other.

In a responsible and responsive professional community, we will find teachers consulting research and employing teaching strategies that work effectively for the particular children they teach. Shelly Harwayne, principal of the Manhattan New School, a public elementary school in the heart of New York City, reports that she is often asked, especially by the press, whether her award-winning inner-city school is a whole language school or a phonics school. She invites the press to visit and they, after visiting classes and finding they are still unable to determine if it is a whole language or phonics school, ask her again: "What kind of reading program does this school have?" Her answer is that if she has 40 children in her school who need special help in learning to read, then she has 40 reading programs, each one identified by the name of a child and each one drawing what is most needed by a particular child from whatever bodies of research and teaching strategies happen to work most effectively for this particular child at this particular moment.

Our profession, as seen from inside teachers' lounges, in the conversations of professionals, and in the presentations and workshops at conferences, is not a bloody battleground of competing ideas, but it has been made to appear so by a press that is hungry for dramatic stories and by impatient policy makers and a frustrated public looking for the same kind of simple answers that popular opinion often demands—answers that offer both scapegoats and saviors. In such a climate of public opinion, we should not be surprised to see legislation attempting to mandate what has been touted as saving instruction based on what has been advertised as "reliable, scientific" research and discounting, if not outlawing, the instructional methods and research studies mistakenly associated with a perceived, though mythical failure. The true ideological battleground for our profession, then, is not in the field where teacher-educators and teachers debate about the most effective teaching strategies, nor is it in the labs and research sites where scholars offer different theoretical perspectives, different methodological procedures, and competing findings. Disagreements in these arenas can and do lead to dialogue and thereby to the advancement of learning.

The battleground on which we are obliged to make our stand is the political battleground where we are losing ground to policy makers and legislators who seek to usurp the professional authority that belongs to teachers and professional educators in matters having to do with curriculum, teaching methodology, and materials. What business do legislators in California or in Congress have in deciding on an approved curriculum for inservice programs for teachers of reading? What moral or ethical or intellectual justification can they offer for arrogating to themselves the authority to declare, with respect to a field of specialized learning, that one research paradigm and one set of research findings is valid and all others invalid, particularly when the world's most widely respected and most extensively published scholars in the field are engaged in a continuing scholarly debate on those very questions?

Collegial Responsibility

That legislators have been encouraged by a handful of reading researchers to act with such usurpacious arrogance is much to the discredit of those researchers, though it may testify more to their naivete than their vulnerability to the attractions of power or the temptations of consulting fees and royalties. Yet, surely, they must see, or we must ask them to recognize, that there is something deeply wrong, professionally and ethically, when one group of researchers in an academic field supports a congressional bill that declares other respected scholars in the field—including many of the most distinguished and revered figures in literacy studies—figures like Shirley Brice Heath and Judith Green and Gordon Wells, scholars whose work has appeared in our most distinguished journals—unacceptable as sources of knowledge or expertise. As a matter of principle having to do with academic freedom (not to mention respect for colleagues), all scholars in the field of literacy studies, regardless of what research paradigms or teaching practices, must stand together and call in one voice for the deletion of any clause in any piece of legislation that has the effect of declaring any group of professionally respected scholars as undeserving of professional respect or attention by virtue of their intellectual orientation. If ethnographic researchers and constructivist theories of learning can be stigmatized today, then behaviorists can be stigmatized tomorrow.

The same arguments that apply to colleagues who are close to the seats of current political power must also, of course, apply to the rest of us who wield other sorts of power. The officers and staff and program organizers of NCTE and other professional organizations in the language arts must be scrupulous not to exercise power in program planning or publication decisions that will have the effect of marginalizing or discounting quantitative research or findings that favor skill-oriented instruction over a more constructivist model, or any intellectually responsible group of researchers, merely because of their scholarly orientation. The rule of charity and collegial respect must apply to all members of the academic community. We must all resist any official or tacit policy that declares any school of professionally respectable scholarship (by which I mean work supported by professional associations and published in scholarly journals, and so on) as officially incorrect. That is the road to totalitarian thinking whether on the left or right.

How Can We Respond to Current Political Outrages?

How can we respond to the misdirected policies enacted or threatened by presumably well-meaning legislatures or to the misguided understanding represented by popular opinion? Surely, we can and must communicate with our legislators to represent our opposition to laws that would interfere with the right of educators to engage in their professional work according to standards set within their profession. We can also write letters to editors and speak out clearly at public forums. It is a fact that even a little bit of lobbying can make a difference in shaping policy. It is also a fact that, in many states, if not in the federal government, policy is presently being shaped largely by the efforts of pressure groups who represent a narrow and repressive conception of learning—what Freire (1970) called the banking model—and with a matching view of reading as nothing more than pronunciation and information retrieval. In the meantime, a more literate public and the professional community in education remain largely silent, disheartened by the drift of political opinion, and feeling, as the not-silent Ken Goodman has described it, alluding to a story he has circulated on e-mail networks, that in such a climate of repression "we have to learn to live under water" (K. Goodman, personal communication, November 12, 1997).

But why, as a profession (though with notable exceptions), are we as silent as we have been—especially those of us who are specialists in the arts of language? What are teachers doing while the representatives of educational *Gradgrindism*[3] and cultural paranoia appear to be controlling public discourse? They are teaching, of course. If we are middle school or secondary school English teachers, we are teaching 150 to 200 students each day, assigning them papers to write that we must read and respond to, preparing lessons, reading professional journals, re-reading the literature we must teach and other literature we might want to teach, attending faculty meetings, meeting with parents, supervising student publications, and, perhaps, spending some time with our own families. If we are elementary teachers, we are lucky to have a bathroom break all day, and our day will probably start early and end late to make room for the hours of preparation and inservice that are required of us to prepare lessons for children at various levels of skill. On top of all this, we must keep ourselves current on teaching theory and methods and materials in everybody else's academic specialty. No group of professionals works harder than good teachers do. To ask them, as well, to become active political lobbyists so that they might resist one more attempt at telling them how to carry out their professional responsibilities seems almost obscene.

Good teachers know, furthermore, that we have always had to "live under water." The current repressive cycle in education is merely another cycle that will pass and good teachers will go on struggling, in spite of institutional obstacles, to do what, in their professional judgment, is best for their students. Even in what might be seen as a permissive rather than a repressive political climate, good teachers have had to live under water. The Superintendent who, this year, banned an inservice program because someone had suggested that it was too whole language, might, a few years ago, have banned the teaching of the alphabet or any kind of teaching of spelling or vocabulary (as many administrators apparently did in California in that state's prior incarnation as a state) that embraced a constructivist model of learning.

Top-down directions for professional teachers—no matter how well-intended or how solidly based on theory—will not work and are almost guaranteed to be intellectually reductive and pedagogically simplistic. No formula for teaching can be allowed to substitute for a teacher's own professional judgment exercised in the context of a particular classroom with particular students at particular moments. What we need from school boards and state and federal education agencies is not better models of teaching and learning to be dictated to teachers, but more respect for the professional judgment of classroom teachers and the funds to provide teachers with time and resources for participating in intensive and intellectually powerful professional development programs (like the National Writing Project) that are built on respect for teachers as well as respect for research, which is to say all professionally honored research.

If, as a profession, we must lobby our legislatures, let us lobby for the right of teachers to practice their profession without the interference of non-educators in matters of curriculum, teaching methods, and materials or research methodologies.

Let policy makers, including legislatures and school boards, set general goals for public schools defined perhaps by some vision of an educated citizenry and then let them provide schools with adequate material resources to do the job of helping students acquire such an education. Let them protect teachers and schools against the fickleness of public opinion and the partisanship of political pressure groups, rather than subject education to their intellectually capricious tyranny.

The genius of the American Constitution and Bill of Rights, I suspect, resides less in how they institutionalize the principle of democratic elections and majority rule (which characterized many earlier governments including some of the Swiss cantons of the sixteenth and seventeenth century) than in the permanent protections they offer to minorities and to individuals and institutions against the changeable will of the majority. Thus, religion is protected from government interference and so is the press, no matter how displeased the majority of American voters or their representatives might become with the way churches and the press conduct their activities.

The American system of public education seems to me no less critical to the health of the nation than the institution of a free press. Nor does it seem to me any less in need of protection against well-intentioned legislators and misguided majorities that would seek to serve their own political or ideological ends through the control of curricular content, teaching methods, or texts. Indeed, in recent years, in many cities and states, we have seen processes as basic as textbook selection become political spectacles featuring power contests between various groups of parents and political stakeholders, rather than thoughtful processes of deliberation among professionals about the materials that would most effectively serve legitimate educational aims. It is time to rescue education, not only from the politicians who are endlessly seeking to "save" it, but from the fickle fashions of public opinion. It is time to offer to schools and to teachers something like constitutional protections so that they may work in the service of a well-informed professional vision without being subject to sabotage at every turn by the latest fetish of one or another political party or pressure group.

This does not mean that educators should not be accountable to the publics they serve. Protecting educators from interference from school boards and legislatures would, in fact, make them more rather than less accountable to the public and to the elected but changing bodies that fund and therefore will always constrain what schools can do.

Presently, legislative bodies and elected boards of education with members who serve for a few years hold enormous authority to dictate policy and practices, but they are rarely still in office, available to be held accountable when the results of failed policies finally become evident. And almost all policies created in response to popular fashions eventually do fail.

Later this year, NCTE plans to join with a number of other professional organizations in a Congress on Public Education. Let us propose that the agenda for this congress include discussion of the problem of how to balance the responsibility of legislatures and school boards to oversee education with their equal responsibility to protect education from becoming a hostage in ideological and political battles. Let us specifically explore mechanisms, including legislation, to protect schools from the sort of legislative and public interference that has created such uncertainty and so threatened both the richest traditions and the most intellectually progressive ideas in public education. If it seems doubtful that our richest traditions could be in jeopardy (along with our most progressive ideas) visit Florida, where legislators and other policy makers are proposing, in the name of educational utility, the marginalization of literary study, so that literature will be taught only in elective classes, while required English classes focus only on reading practical texts like warrantees, scientific reports, and directions.

Will our next political campaign have to be in Florida to stop legislators from enacting a policy that could be supported only by persons with extremely limited experiences with literature and little understanding of the nature of literary study? That such semi-literate persons, however well-intentioned or morally uptight, could be in a position to dictate curriculum or educational policy in English studies is a perversion of democratic pnnciples and an absurdity of the kind that a Renaissance rhetorician might refer to as an outrage against nature—equivalent to the idea that the foot should rule the head or that "the bounded waters should lift their bosoms higher than the shores . . . and the rude son should strike his father dead" (*Troilus and Cressida*, 1, 3, 111–115).

I had thought, for a time, to suggest that NCTE actually initiate a campaign for a Constitutional Amendment to be known as the Academic Freedom Amendment. And I do want to put the idea on the table as a proposal for some distant and utopian future, a consummation devoutly to be wished, perhaps, yet so implausible a goal in our own time as to commend itself only to our imaginations. Nevertheless, we can and should, at this time of an approaching new millennium, make a case to responsible and thoughtful legislators in state and federal bodies for some mechanism that would allow education to operate in a zone more free of political interference than is now our sorry condition.

In the meantime, we can all take heart from noting that NCTE has launched what we are calling a Reading Research Strike Force consisting of some 15 internationally respected scholars who will be issuing White Papers and preparing briefing documents in response to distorted accounts of scientific research that have been widely circulated by lobbyists who speak for various political and ideological pressure groups. Our straight-talking and illuminating documents will be widely available to classroom teachers for use in local schools and communities. It is also the case that, even as we speak, two important documents are being released from two different federally funded research groups that seriously challenge and even discredit many of the conclusions drawn by phonics-crazed policy makers based on NICHD (National Institute of Child Health and Human Development) research and specifically on the widely circulated report synthesizing 30 years of NICHD research—a report that has powerfully influenced the intrusive and misguided reading policies adopted in California and Texas, and by the House of Representatives.

What changes in political opinion might follow upon strong research reports calling into question the research upon which politicians and much of the public have mounted their calls for repressive reforms? Would it be reasonable to assume that the growing number of studies discrediting the research base for educationally intrusive legislation on reading, will now lead political leaders to acknowledge that they might have been guilty of premature legislation or that, in future, it might be wiser to protect schools and teachers from politically charged intrusions rather than try to regulate them legislatively in matters of teaching methods and materials? It is doubtful that any such concession will be forthcoming. Yet the new studies may be preparing the way for a political sea change in which those who have been living under water may be able to surface for a short breath of fresh air.

Notes

1. This is a crisis that some of our most thoughtful colleagues have demonstrated has been largely invented by the popular press.

2. Most of whom appear to be financially linked to textbooks and publishing companies whose reading programs claim to be based on quantifiable research.

3. Gradgrind, Thomas, an intensely matter-of-fact, utilitarian hardware merchant from Dickens' novel *Hard Times*, a character whose name has come to mean philistinism.

References

Freire, P. (1970). *Pedagogy of the oppressed.* New York: Continuum.

Goodman, K. (1997, November 8). Untitled e-mail message. Circulated to National Reading Council listserve: *NRCEMAIL@ASUVM. INREASU.* EDU.

Pound, E. (1960). *ABC of reading.* New York: New Directions. (Original work published in 1934).

10 Literacy Education as a Political Act

Diane Stephens

In *Zen and the Art of Motorcycle Maintenance* (1974), the central character, Phaedrus, describes a motorcycle by dividing it into "component assemblies" (e.g., a power assembly and a running assembly) and into "functions." He divides each of these further and explains each part. He then comments on his description, pointing out aspects of it that are not, at first, obvious. He notes, for example, that "if you were to go to a motorcycle-parts department and ask them for a feedback assembly" (or any of these parts):

> they wouldn't know what . . . you were talking about. They don't split it up that way. No two manufacturers ever split it up quite the same way and every mechanic is familiar with the problem of the part you can't buy because the manufacturer considers it a part of something else (79).

What Phaedrus wants the reader to understand is that different people divide the world up differently. Different people have different ways of viewing the motorcycle, and, by extension, the world. In order to make sense of these multiple realities, Phaedrus believes that we need to take a step back from descriptions and perceptions to be able to see that what he calls a "knife" that is used to create categories and ways of seeing the world. He explains that this knife is

> an intellectual scalpel so swift and sharp you sometimes don't see it moving. You get the illusion that all these parts are just there and are being named as they exist. But they can be named quite differently and organized quite differently depending on how the knife moves. . . . It is important to see this knife for what it is and not to be fooled into thinking that motorcycles or anything else are the way they are

---

Reprinted from *Practicing What We Know,* edited by Constance Weaver.

just because the knife happened to cut it that way. It is important to concentrate on the knife itself . . . (79).

He also cautions us to remember that categories are inherent in any description and those descriptions, those categories, exist because someone, wielding a metaphorical knife, created them. He advises us not only to step back far enough to see the knife but also to see the knife holder.

I don't know enough about the author, Robert Pirsig, to explain why he wrote *Zen and the Art of Motorcycle Maintenance*. I suspect his motivation was personal and philosophical. I do know that my motivation, in choosing to tell this part of his story here, is political. I am worried about how decisions are being made in reading education, and by and for whom they are being made.

Since the early 1980s, various stakeholders have been debating what "should" be happening in classrooms in the name of reading instruction. Using Phaedrus' metaphor of the motorcycle parts, it is as if Person A walks into a store and tries to buy a part, as Phaedrus named it. The store owner, Person B, says he does not have that part. Person A argues that he should have. B says he should not. From B's point of view, the stock is organized in the best possible way. From A's point of view, A's way of organizing and categorizing is better. In reading research, the argument is similar. Researcher A asks for standardized test results from Researcher B as "proof" of his or her findings and Researcher B says "I don't have any and I don't believe I need them and besides I wasn't trying to prove but to understand" and Researcher A says, "Well, you should have them and you do need them and it is your job to prove" and Person B says, "No, I shouldn't and I don't and it isn't." So then A says and B says . . .

Just as Pirsig/Phaedrus wants us to step back from his description of the motorcycle, I believe that teachers need to step back from these debates. When we do so, we can see that each debater is a knife holder and each has divided up reading and reading instruction in different ways. This happens because each debater holds different beliefs about what reading is, how it can be understood, and how reading instruction can or should be improved. The debaters also divide up research and knowledge in different ways. They hold different beliefs about what kinds of questions are worth asking, what kind of data address those questions, and how to make sense of the data. When we are able to see the knives and the knife holders, we are able to juxtapose our beliefs with theirs and, in so doing, critically reflect on our own beliefs. We wield a knife and create a world that makes sense to us and to the children for whom we are responsible.

In the foreword to *Reconsidering a Balanced Approach to Reading,* I argued that teachers need to form their own beliefs and the argument I gave there and above makes it sound as if I think they should do so because I simply think it is a "good idea." But it is more than a good idea. It is a political necessity. The stakes in the debate have escalated. The debate used to focus on what was known about reading instruction and what were the implications of that knowledge for classroom practice. In the last few years, however, the focus has shifted. The debate still includes conversation about what we know and what teachers should do, but it has broadened to include a new, and to my mind, dangerous, third topic: Who or what should decide and ensure that teachers do what they "should" be doing?

What is interesting about this question is that when you step back from it, it becomes clear that the only people who ask this question are those who believe that they know what teachers "should" be doing (that is, they believe there is one right answer—theirs); that something or someone needs to tell teachers what to do; and that someone or something needs to be in place to ensure that teachers will do as they are told. These question-askers have "fixated belief" about what teachers "should" be doing by reviewing research, and, sometimes, conducting their own. In their review of the literature, however, like most of us, they disregard that which they do not consider to be valid. Going back to the store analogy, it is as if Researcher A decided that Researcher B's work was not informative because it did not contain the parts that Researcher A wanted. In the example above, the work did not have standardized test scores. So Researcher A does not "count" the research of B when drawing conclusions about the findings from the literature review. Researcher B, again with the best of intentions, does the same thing: She or he does not include the findings from studies that she or he does not consider informative.

What makes this confusing is that each of these researchers then holds a press conference (or writes an article or book) and makes statements about what "the research" shows. Because each researcher has discarded some studies and included others, their statements conflict. What makes this scenario frightening is that some of the people listening to these announcements (or reading the texts) believe that the researcher they are hearing/reading is right and that the other researcher is wrong. Convinced of the right path to follow and believing that, without a mandate, teachers will not follow the right path, some of the question-askers join forces with legislators and businesspersons and attempt, and sometimes succeed, in getting their "right" answer made into a law to which all teachers are held accountable. In California, for example, it is not legal to use Goals 2000 funds for programs that encourage students to use context to figure out words instead of decoding words fluently. Meanwhile, the State Board of Education removed from the recommended texts list the materials published by the Wright Group and Rigby, both of whom publish extensive collections of predictable books for young readers.

Other people, similarly convinced that they know what is right for teachers, follow different paths. Some, for example, believe that literacy instruction could be improved if university professors came together and detailed what they thought good reading instruction should look like in the elementary classroom. Sometimes they do this by helping to construct national reading tests. David Pearson (1996), for example, seems to envision beliefs about reading education along a numbered continuum with everyone from 2 to 9 joined in a 15-year-long debate. During that time period, the radical left (the 1s) have been rallying for their cause and forming teacher support groups while the radical right (the 10s) have been collaborating with non-educators (businesspersons and legislators) to build a structure for reading education that can be legislatively mandated and that excludes everyone else on the continuum. Pearson believes that over these 15 or so years, the "center" has shifted, positively, to the left, but believes, because of the work done by the far right group, that the shift is about to swing in the other direction. He therefore suggests that educators like himself get together to detail a "balanced approach," a common ground "in the middle." In a recent article (1996), he describes what a "balanced" reading program should look like and calls for other educators to join him in the "Radical Middle."

The people who *are not* asking the question, Who or what should decide and ensure that teachers do what they "should" be doing?, are worried about the enormous pressure being put on teachers by those who *are* asking the question. They worry about the laws that are being passed, about the tests that are being written, and about the "middle ground" that is being proposed for teachers by others. Connie Weaver, like me, is one of those worriers. She believes that legislation and national examinations and prescribed "balanced" approaches serve to silence the voices and diminish the power of teachers. Her response is to make public a knowledge base so that teachers and other stakeholders can make informed decisions about their practices. *Practicing What We Know* and *Reconsidering a Balanced Approach to Reading* represent her attempt to do just that. In the first volume, she gathered together articles she felt would inform our understanding of the reading process, learning to read, and the teaching of reading and she particularly included those voices that currently are not being heard by legislators and others who think they should tell teachers how to teach reading. In this volume, she tries to show the readers what practice looks like when it is grounded in that understanding. In order to encourage teachers to broaden their conversations about literacy development and education, she has included some articles that differ somewhat from her own perspective.

David and Connie, however, like the rest of us, cannot stand outside their own reality. Despite his good intentions, David's solution, his "balanced approach," is not so much a response to the debate as a restatement of the position he has consistently held within it. The same can be said of these two volumes. Especially in her own articles, Connie offers a solution but it is not basically a new solution. Her solution, like David's, is a restatement and refinement of the position that she consistently has held. In their writing, David and Connie have made it clear how they have solved the tensions they have faced and how they believe others should or might solve theirs.

As teachers, then, we need to step back and see David and Connie and all other participants as knife holders who are constructing worlds. We need to see their texts as documents that describe the world they have constructed. Doing so gives us the freedom to act independently and prevents us from being held hostage by the debate and by the texts we read. If we cannot do so, if we cannot see knives and knife holders and see instead only "experts" with right answers, we become trapped in the illusion that ultimately there is one truth, one reality, one solution. It becomes too easy for others to prescribe for us what they want us to do in the world they are trying to construct around us.

If, on the other hand, we want teachers (and not legislators or businesspersons or presidents or testing companies or college professors) to be in charge of teaching, we can follow neither Connie nor David nor any of the others who urge us down a particular path. Nor can we sit quietly on the sidelines waiting for the debate to somehow be resolved. What we must do instead is leave the sidelines, accept that there are multiple realities, seize the knife, and construct our own reality. As in the first volume, it is my hope, and Connie's, that this text will help you do so.

Postscript: I have suggested that educators who read these volumes (or any other information about education), accept that there are multiple realities and try to see the knife and the knife holder. To that end, I'm adding this postscript so that I might more easily be seen. I've tried, throughout this introduction, to keep myself visible in the text. I used the phrase "I think" or "I believe" whenever possible even though I knew the editor might hate those phrases and want to delete all instances. I did so because I wanted to keep myself as visible as possible as a knife wielder. I want you to be able to see that, on David's continuum (the one I assumed he had), I am on the far left. I am not interested in joining the debate. I don't believe that the debate is resolvable because I believe that individuals cannot step outside their own realities. I have therefore done what I can to separate myself from it. I believe that teachers should do likewise. I believe that instead of either becoming participants or remaining on the sidelines, teachers should make their own informed decisions and stand firm enough in their knowledge base to weather the storm of the debate. I believe all of us as teachers should stand firm enough so that no one can make us fit into pre-established structures. I believe in strength in numbers and I believe we will hit a critical mass. At that point, teachers will simply have become too strong and it will be fruitless for legislators and senators and presidents and test makers to try to tell us what to do. Teaching will have become a profession and it will be the teachers themselves that have made it so. Along the way, like Connie and David, I seize opportunities to get my voice heard in the conversation and to help make room for the voices of others. Because this is my world view, my reality, I ended this introduction, and the earlier one, suggesting that others do the same. It is the only reality I know. From my perspective, it is the only chance we have.

Works Cited

Pearson, P. D. (1996). Reclaiming the center. In M. Graves, P. van der Broek, & B. Taylor (Eds.), *The first R.* New York: Teachers College Press.
Pirsig, R. (1974). *Zen and the art of motorcycle maintenance.* New York: Morrow.

11 Conflicting Interests: Critical Theory Inside Out

Roberta J. Herter

Introduction

"To be or not to be. That *was* the question. We're going to change the question." Victor, a seventeen-year-old African American male, set the scene for the first night of his English class at Henry Ford High School in Detroit.[1] Victor had chosen "to avoid the hassles" of day school, as he put it, by enrolling in night school. He was well-known and well-liked among the three hundred fifty night school students, many of whom had also dropped out of the crowded, anonymous day school of over two thousand students. Along with seven other night school students, Victor had volunteered to take part in a special semester-long theater workshop in collaboration with a college class from the University of Michigan. With his turn of Hamlet's phrase, Victor eagerly introduced himself to Sally, Susan, and Paul, three of the college students who came to his night school classroom once a week on Wednesday evenings during the winter semester of 1994. The college students were white, middle class to affluent, enrolled in a 300-level English course entitled "Theater and Social Change." Like Victor, the high school students were working-class African Americans enrolled in a required night school English course and quite different from the college students with whom they would collaborate. The goal of the project for the college

---

Reprinted from Chapter 7 of *Literacy and Democracy,* edited by Cathy Fleischer and David Schaafsma.

students, as defined by the course description at the university, was to "form small groups to perform, in nontraditional spaces, street, action, and guerrilla theater pieces advocating social change." The goal for the high school students was to substitute something a little different for the traditional American Literature course required for these night school students: English 56, "Theater Workshop."

I had been teaching night school at Henry Ford for ten years when Buzz Alexander, a professor of English at the University of Michigan and an experienced political organizer, began looking for another project site in which to continue his ongoing outreach work. An urban night school class had potential to provide an interesting alternative setting, he suggested. For many high school students, night school has become a viable choice for those who select it as an alternative to mandatory day school. Further expanding choice into course selection for these students, it seemed to us, might mitigate the stigmatizing labels sometimes attached to those who enroll in night school. As well, as both a teacher at the high school and a graduate student at the university, I welcomed the collaboration. From a teacher's perspective the student-to-student interaction promised a unique learning opportunity for my students and for me, and so I viewed the theater project as an invitation for curricular change rather than as an intervention program.

The college students, obviously interested in issues of social change, were encountering authors like Freire for the first time, and they had had minimal real-world experience in settings that were culturally different from their own. Their texts for the course included Kohl's 36 *Children,* Clyde Taylor's *Dangerous Society,* Freire's *Pedagogy of the Oppressed,* Boal's *Theater of the Oppressed,* and Myles Horton's *The Long Haul.* However, as the college students soon discovered, these readings could not quite capture the complexity of the group of students they would meet at the high school; neither had their suburban high schools prepared them for an inner-city classroom.[2]

Not surprisingly, the weekly workshops produced tensions from the beginning—some typical of any classroom encounter and some created by the unique situation this particular collaboration presented. For example, in the process of collaboration, the high school students' interests proved different from the college students'. Victor's opening declaration is characteristic in its implication that the high school students understood theater differently from the social action thrust of the college students' readings and interests. For Victor and others, theater was defined in terms of

its conventions of scripts, characterization, and performance.
Knowledgeable about theater and a regular at Detroit's Attic Theater, Victor's
expectations of the course were that it would emphasize those conventions:
students would read plays, study dramatic form, write scripts in terms of
those conventions and perform scenes. In contrast, the college students
designed a course which emphasized such elements as warm-up exercises,
theater games, journal writing, and oral script composition based in the
students' own lives, culminating in "performance pieces." Victor had
intended to use his writing ability in the theater class but was repeatedly
defeated by the college students' insistence, instead, on extemporaneous
performance. In their writing and conversations with me, the high school
students expressed their expectation that the theater project would teach
them principles of acting, would give them a chance to perform and have
fun, and would allow them to meet new people. In contrast, the college
students expressed a desire to learn from the high school students, to "help"
them in whatever way possible, and to make a difference in their lives
through the theater encounter. In this paper, I will explore how these
differing expectations and backgrounds played out in this collaborative
venture.

From the perspective of the college students, the project began with
theoretical readings rather than with an immersion in the culture of the night
school. The primary text for English 319 was Augusto Boal's *Theatre of the
Oppressed* (TO), a polemic analyzing western aesthetic philosophy while
explicating political theater. Boal's vision of theater is based on Freire's
broader ideological perspective. Born of the political struggles in Latin
America during the 1960s, its technique is dramatic confrontation in order to
display everyday complicity in various forms of oppression. As I viewed and
reviewed videotapes of the students' weekly meetings and transcribed their
dialogue into text, I began to wonder how the underlying critical theory of
the project supported the college students in their attempts to make visible
the complicated structures of an everyday life they were only beginning to
see. As these college students struggled to negotiate the high school students'
expectations of theater while at the same time trying to enact Boal's
ideological theater, they were faced with the complex dynamic of being
students from a powerful elite institution attempting to collaborate within the
institutional constraints of an urban public school.[3] While the collaborative
constraints represented one form of conflict for the students, they were
additionally constrained by Freire's categorical constructions of "oppressor"
and "oppressed," which framed the project.

As a practitioner of critical pedagogies, I began writing this paper with the intention of describing the students' interactive processes in an attempt to identify the sources of their conflicts. What I found was a pattern of discourse which threatened equitable negotiation. Selected excerpts from the student interactions will illustrate features of the project discourse, which not only revealed sources of conflict but identified broader conflicting interests between the two groups of students.

The Project Begins

At the outset of the project I had discussed with both groups of students that I was interested in looking at how they worked together in producing their final performance pieces. Each of these sessions during the winter of 1994 was videotaped by a stationary video camera which the high school students set up in the corner of the classroom before their sessions began. I was teaching a class next door, and the project workshop was designed to be conducted by students for students in an adjacent classroom.

During the course of the semester, I was able to review the videotapes with the high school students to discuss their reactions to the class. Transcripts of the videotapes created a text that further enabled the high school students and me to view and discuss their workshops. Their initial take on theater, as Victor interpreted it, was a theater of expression, of imagination, of re-creation. In contrast, they saw the college students as focusing on a more overtly political construction of theater. While Boal's TO presented an opportunity for critical self-reflection, the high school students were not equally informed of its methods, and consequently found their lived experience subject to exposure rather than having their more technical concerns, such as the conventions of scriptwriting, addressed. For example, after two weeks of introductory theater games designed to loosen up and engage students in the process of creating scenes, the college students began asking Victor, Diego, Eve, and the others to talk about themselves. The invitation was met with confusion by the high school students who were unclear how their lives and theater came together, but they were willing to try. The first scenes the high school students put together included depictions of police brutality, rape, domestic violence, and substance abuse, based in their lived experiences. The college students' lives, in contrast, went unexposed as they participated in the scenes by playing roles assigned them by the high school students.

Contributing to this issue of unequal exposure were a number of occasions of disjunctures of discourse. As members of different discourse communities, the college students' interactions with the high school students produced a discourse defined by the negotiation necessary to accomplish weekly work. On the surface, their working discourse was characterized by the push and pull of classroom conversation, but when I looked deeper, I saw a discourse revealing some of the complexities of theoretically based cross-cultural communication in a school setting.[4]

Global vs. Local Questions

In attempting to locate the sources of tension in the students' interactions, I viewed and reviewed both the videotapes and their transcripts. As I mentioned above, the college students faced a dual dilemma by having to negotiate the theoretical constraints of Boal's theater with the conflicting interests of the high school students. They were, as Mady Schutzman points out, like all North American practitioners of Boal's theater, "working with groups to which they themselves do not belong, and thus represent, ironically, the very element of oppression the exclusion of which the group is founded upon" (141). Despite this dilemma and for all their differences, their common identities as students seemed to enable their dialogue and foster a commitment to the performative aspects of their work. In fact they did produce final performance pieces at the end of the project. The most persistent feature emerging from and intruding upon the students' interactions, however, was their different use of questions. My focus on the use of questions developed out of a close reading of the transcribed texts in response to the high school students' belief that they were not being heard when they suggested scenes for the workshop. The dialogues which I reviewed demonstrated an intricate form of resistance by the high school students when questions were used—by both groups—for multiple purposes and for achieving multiple goals.

Typically the conventions of asking questions in school settings are to elicit information, to check students' knowledge and understandings, and to pose problems for students to solve. Those teacherly uses, however, were notably absent in the interactions of these two groups of students. During the course of their interactions over the seventeen-week semester, the high school students generated almost twice as much talk in real time as measured by the text generated in transcripts of their videotaped interactions with the college students, but the college students asked twice as many questions as the high school students. However, numbers alone don't reveal the way questions were used by the students to inquire, speculate, philosophize, challenge the project's purpose, express desires, control opposition, silence one another, and assert authority.

Victor, Diego, and Eve stood apart from the other high school students as they used questions to undermine the college students' intention of exposing the high school students' lives for critical, reflexive examination. Through their resistance, the high school students not only reiterated their understanding of theater as imaginative play, but they also contrasted the everyday level of their lives with an imagined ideal. In a form of Heideggerian self-consciousness, the high school students elected to act out ideal lives in order to create and take on new characters often connected to their own lives, but occasionally in opposition to their lived experience (Heidegger 82–83). As I will explain in a moment, this insistence served in opposition to the college students' vision of this class.

By contrast the college students used questions very differently, at times in ways theoretically inconsistent with liberatory pedagogy. These questions became a way of controlling the behavior of the high school youth, limiting their responses, and contradicting the declaration of shared authority that the high school youth had rejected. Eve spoke for the high school group when she announced, "We talk freer when you all not here 'cause you all older." This prompted Sally, one of the college students to respond, "This is *our* class. We're all teachers here." In fact, some of the high school students were older than the college students, but Eve's message attempted to communicate something more complex than age. For example, one week when the college students were absent, Eve served as facilitator of the group, using the occasion to compare medical treatment she had received at two clinics. When the college students returned the following week and she tried to pick up both the thread of the conversation and the role she had taken on, she was ignored. Instead of even inquiring about what had happened in their absence, the college students began the class with "Well, let's get started," almost as if they hadn't been absent the week before. The stated shared authority of the group faced similar repeated challenges within the critical theoretical framework when the college students seemed frustrated in their attempt to respond openly to the high school students. The focus on lived experience suitable for performance put the college students in the position of judging what life experiences were valid and available as products of classroom conversation.

Changing the Question: Diego and Victor

Sally, Paul, and Susan's plans for developing scenes continually bumped up against some of the expressed desires of the high school students. When it came to developing scenes depicting significant events in their lives, some of the high school students elected to envision scenes from their imaginations. Both Victor and Diego argued that they didn't want to be themselves in scenes. They felt that they were already familiar with their own experience and wanted to try on new ways of being. Diego in particular wanted to imagine a role in which he reacted differently to a situation where he knew he would be forced into a fight. He imagined a character named Silvio, a tough kid, always ready to fight—unlike the real Diego who prided himself on talking his way out of trouble. For him the freedom to put himself in a real-life situation, but as an imagined self, allowed him to try on new ways of being which he said would permit him "to think differently." Sally, however, offered resistance to Diego's conceptualization of the scene. Through her questions, she remained faithful to Boal's political theater, but obstructed Diego's search for real life alternatives to his existing way of dealing with conflict.

When Diego proposed exploring alternatives to fighting in a real-life situation by examining his own first response with an imagined possible response, the exchange went like this (the college students' voices are in bold print):

> *Paul:* **One of the things that's important about acting is that you use your life to fuel it. You can't . . .**
>
> *Diego:* That's why I want to be different, a totally different person in a role than I am in reality, do something I've never done before. I want to be a totally different person. Somebody talk about the way I look, I don't fight. I don't really care what you think, but Silvio does. That's why I picked Silvio because me and him is two different characters. He wouldn't even be sitting here. He wouldn't be in this group. His bike would be up on Schoolcraft. He would be meeting. Silvio cares what other people think about him. I don't. Silvio end up being bad at school.
>
> *Sally:* **Isn't that still too close?**
>
> *Paul:* **Could . . .**
>
> *Sally:* **Ebony, what do you think of the situation? Put Silvio in the situation.**

Diego: . . .

Sally: **Because it's so powerful. What do you think? You want to do something completely different?**

Diego: No, 'cause like I said, an actor is his work.

Sally: **Ebony, do you like that?**

(Diego turns his back and walks away from Sally.)

Diego's insistence on trying on a new and different persona met resistance from Paul and Sally in the form of questions, but he was resolute in identifying himself as an "actor." Diego reasoned that the character of Silvio was so unlike himself, that Silvio wouldn't even participate in this group. Diego emphasized Silvio's difference by contrasting his combative nature with Diego's more cooperative character. In addition, Diego acknowledged that Silvio "was bad in school" and that he probably wouldn't be involved in this project. Diego offered these rationalizations to persuade Sally and Paul that his choice was legitimate and based on his understanding of theater and the character of Silvio that he had created, but his suggestions were rejected. The gap between what Diego chose as his form of self-representation conflicted with the genre constraints of theater as the college students constructed it. In part, this gap occurred because of the lack of shared knowledge: Diego had not read Freire, and the college students had not directly shared their understanding of liberatory theater with the high school students. The college students had not adopted an "inclusive or a critical orientation" in their interactions with the high school students (Burbules 111). Their dialogue illustrates the more "separate knowing" that Belenky and her co-authors identify. This lack of understanding and rejection of the high school students' choice of characters as different from themselves occurred throughout the project: as you will see shortly, Victor, for example, experienced the same diversion when he insisted on imagining life as a Colombian immigrant.

Paul and Sally searched for ways to bring the students' lives into the scenes the group was preparing, but they didn't support the students when they chose to reimagine their lives, to think alternately of their own lived experience or to invent what Markus and Nurius refer to as "possible selves." Neither Victor nor Diego needed any prompting in their imaginative turn. Both students argued their cases persuasively; however, Paul and Sally were caught between the project's goals being appropriated by the high school students and enforcing their conceptualization of the project—or negotiating a compromise. While other possibilities for defining mutually agreed-upon goals could have resolved the conflict, the absence of negotiated differences prevented all of the students from expressing their personal constructions of the project.

On another occasion Diego searched for an alternative portrayal of himself, this time as a character distanced from the reality of a friend's recent death. Sally and Paul again attempted to persuade him to reconsider his choice. Diego held firm, and justified his choice.

Sally: How about something doing with school?

Diego: I thought of a dialogue.

Paul: Do you want to do a monologue or do a dialogue?

Diego: You know how you get all of a sudden?

Sally: What happened to you this week, uh, you had a very strong reaction to that and I think if you wanted to, maybe portray that?

Paul: Why not?

Diego: No, [shaking head] no, uh I mean if this was another time, but the way the situation is now, it'd be kind of hard. You know how if you were doing a play with a death in it? Now if you had just been to a funeral, and you went to play that you just went to a funeral, it be kind of hard 'cause you know you'd see no one but that person you saw in that casket, and then you want to be in a play? That would have a big impact on your mind. You know, you'd think, dang!

Sally: Do you think it would help you work through some of these feelings?

Diego: Honestly what I told I didn't want to throw it away, but basically in the back of my mind, calming myself down, having a fantasy or dream because I know her as a friend.

Paul: You could . . .

Diego: I want to be a totally different person in a role, and then a totally different person in reality because when you think about it, if I'm going to be a punk like Silvio, I don't want to be like that. Silvio end up being bad. See? That's why I picked Silvio because me and him is two different people.

Diego held his ground, but Sally and Paul's questions attempted to coerce him into making a choice between a scene out of his own life or one in which he reimagined his own life building on his sense of possibility. Interestingly, though, it was because of their questions that Diego found himself defending his creation of Silvio's character.

Like Diego, Victor had an interest in performing, as indicated by his interpretation of Hamlet's soliloquy. He was the most enthusiastic participant among the high school students, first to enter the classroom each night, eager to set up the camera and do a check by taping himself sending messages to me. Throughout the semester Victor both facilitated and frustrated the group's efforts by consistently resisting the attempts of the college students to persuade him to abandon his imagined character for one based on his own life, when in fact, Victor saw the complex relationship of drug dealing and stereotyping young black males as his own life dilemma. Victor held fast to his idea and developed it into a performance by the end of the semester. How did he manage to resist the influence of the college students, and how did he persist in the creation of his imagined character? A partial answer rests in Victor's understanding of theater and his appropriation of the college students' agenda.

Victor not only knew what he wanted to perform, he expected the college students to support his choice and show him how to create his character. What he met instead was resistance to the role he created of a Colombian importer who is mistaken for a druglord. The following scene was developed and performed by Victor at the final performance. The questions raised and implied by the piece indicate Victor's interest in stereotypical representations of men in his community.

Victor's Druglord Scene

Real Time: Three minutes, twenty seconds

Setting: An office in a large city

Victor: One thing that troubles me as well as all people on this earth at one time or another. My problem is stereotypes. Why do people judge each other negatively and treat each other differently just because of the way they look or the things they do or the things they wear. This is sort of hard for me to explain to you, Sir, but if I could have a moment of your time . . . I can . . .

Sir: (from behind a newspaper) Go on, go on.

Victor: You see, Sir, I came to this country for a business meeting, and I didn't like the things I heard or I saw. I heard things like, "The big drug man is in town" or "Look! That must be the druglord." People even acted afraid of me!

Sir: What?

Victor: You see sir, I run a transport company in Colombia. A man asked another man at a meeting that I attended, what I did for a living. This man told him. I ran a transport company in Colombia. This man treated me bad. He acted strange towards me all because of what I did. I don't understand why he did this, Sir. Tell me why. Why did he do this?

Sir: Uh, uh. Well, uh, I don't know.

Victor: Well how about the time when I went to the store to buy a candy bar? I saw how the man behind the counter treated these kids. They were nothing but neighborhood kids who just came in from the street. Little urban kids. The man treated them like they were going to steal something.

Sir: Why does that concern you?

Victor: This concerns me because I realize now it's not just the people I deal with, but everybody treats each other differently just because of who they are or where they're from. This man treats these kids just like this just because of where they came from. Everybody's doing this now, it's not just the people I deal with. People cannot survive if we continue to treat each other badly just because of who you are or what color you are or where you came from. Why, Sir, why do people do this? Why?

Sir: Well, uh . . .

Victor: Sir, are you listening? See? (to audience) You all see? Sir is reading the newspaper. A newspaper, a newspaper! I bet it's the media. People let television and newspapers control their minds, tell them what to wear, what they should think. A brown box made of wood and plastic should not decide what you should wear, who you should be friends with, what you should think. It's not right. Then again, the media ain't the same in all countries. There's a lot of difference in countries. Media ain't. Countries, government. What's the same in all countries?

Sir: Yeah, I'm listening.

Susan: (walks through set, grabs Victor's arm pulling him off stage) Time's up.

Victor: But . . .

Susan: Time's up. (continues pulling him off stage)

Victor: (from off stage) Answer me, Sir. Sir. Sir.

Victor's scene depicts his frustration at not engaging answers to his big question: "Why, Sir, why do people do this [stereotyping]?" Victor invokes "Sir" as an unresponsive moral authority. In their self-conscious and deliberate choice to fictionalize their character in opposition to the "real-life" story the theater project encouraged, both Diego and Victor attempted to find in their imaginations a new identity, a possible self, a moral "I." In so doing, they disclosed and defined themselves ontologically as they sought respect, dignity, and compassion through the lives and life situations of the characters they created.

Where the theater project began for the college students with Freire and Boal's theory of conscientization, for the high school students it began with their imaginings of other ways of being as a way of delving more deeply into their known lives. Thus, the project's purposes were contradictory and complex. In part because the purpose centered on the generation and enactment of theory grounded in the resistance of the high school youth, critical theory, from the outset, supplanted the needs and desires of the theater project participants.

According to Usher and Edwards, "For us, it is about reconfiguring emancipation/oppression in favour of the excluded and oppressed. In this, we need to recognize, however, that the oppressed might also become oppressors, that there is always a danger of simply replacing one totalising, oppressive discourse with another" (213). The college students created scenes which revealed the high school students' lives but didn't implicate themselves equally in the process. The absence of reciprocal openness and inquiry placed the high school students in the vulnerable position as object of a "critical" project.

Questions of Control

Their shared social identity as students was a point of interest and connection where the two diverse groups aligned themselves, and yet they persisted in contradictory constructions of one another. As the two groups of students struggled to identify and negotiate project goals, their interactions revealed other sources of conflict. Again by looking closely at their discourse, some of the less obvious differences between the two groups of students emerged. In order to get a sharper picture of the group's interactions, I narrowed my look at the project by focusing on the discourse of their interactions.

"We're not your teachers, we're all teaching," Sally announced, attempting to equalize her authority by this declaration. The following interaction took place the second week of the course and illustrates the use of questions to silence the high school students.

Paul: **Does anyone have any questions right now, er, like just . . . Anything you want to ask about us or next time?**

Cory: Yeah, which came first, the chicken or the egg?

Victor: The egg.

Sally: **Chicken.**

Paul: **The egg. You said first, you go ahead.**

Victor: Why'd the egg come first? I don't know. I just feel that way, the egg came first.

Cory: Where'd that come from?

Victor: The egg just magically appeared. The eggs just magically appeared?

Cory: Why?

Charity: I believe the chicken came first because when God made earth he put two of every kind on this earth.

Victor: How'd you know there weren't two eggs? How'd you know there weren't two eggs? There could have been two eggs that might have hatched and then there were two chickens.

Eve: No. You . . .

Victor: You know chickens don't just appear, they have to hatch.

Eve: You have to understand. God created the sun and earth first. Then he created people, a man and a woman, nah. Then he created two chickens. . . .

Victor: Does the Bible specifically say God created two chickens? How do you know he didn't create two eggs?

Eve: (raised voice) Read the Bible, boy!

Sally: **Anyone have any other questions? (pause) Can we go around and say names again? I'm Sally.**

Where Cory's question is used to entertain and humor his peers, Sally uses her question to shut down the banter. The high school students could have kept this up for a time, but Sally's two questions allowed her to regain the floor and redirect the conversation.

Power relations in schools are often constructed in terms of teacher/student authority; however, there are other forms of power exerted less visibly and more ambiguously on both teachers and students through a largely bureaucratized system of teaching and learning. Foucault proposes the interrogation of institutional discourses as a way of revealing forms of bureaucratically rationalized domination, while Pierre Bourdieu in *Outline of a Theory of Practice,* "Systems of Education and Systems of Thought," and *Reproduction in Education, Society, and Culture,* argues for the analysis of personal discourse as a way of coming to understand social interactions and power dynamics in interpersonal relations. Each of these can help us rethink the use of questions by the college students, burdened by their cultural and institutional representations as outsiders.

The following exchange revealed another way in which the college students used questions in shaping the high school students' responses. The previous hour had been filled with playfulness and unproductive activity. This led Susan to attempt to get the group back to more focused activity.

Susan: Victor, what do you think?

Victor: Y'all not organized.

Sally: Do you guys think we'll be able to produce a play if we keep working like this?

Ken: No.

Susan: So what helped you last time?

Victor: Like you got to learn to, OK, act it.

Susan: So?

Victor: Just tell me that Jose is about to die.

Sally: That's what we're trying to say.

Eve: And tell us what part to act out. Let them . . . You all didn't say . . . You just tell them. Most plays that you're directing . . . You going to say what you done read. Most people . . . You . . .

Victor: That's not really true though 'cause last week when we went to the play in Ann Arbor. He had to figure out how he was going to act as a gay person. The lady, she was supposed to have that, she was uppity or whatever.

Eve: She didn't tell us, you know how to investigate . . . What the meaning of the investigator? How do a murderer act? How do a murderer think?

Susan: How did you feel when you were playing that role or is that how you would have really acted? What? How do you know that?

Susan's questions served to place blame. A literal reading of Eve's questions, for example, might be interpreted as seeking information; however, in the given context, they are accusatory. Rather than replying with information which would not be an appropriate response here, Susan fires back with a string of questions to again rebuild the floor.

The familiar Freirean notions of power, empowerment, and invention (or the college students' understandings of these notions) conflicted with high school students' expectations of the project. When seen through their eyes, these notions become, in one sense, objects of a theoretical and ideological gaze fixed on them through the college students' understandings of community service as a mode of empowering the high school youth. Through this unintentional "othering," the college students undermined the theoretical foundations of the project with their attempt at "teaching" theater as a form of empowerment to the high school students.

The premature leap to Theater of the Oppressed, without adequate preparation for the high school students to understand how this form of theater is designed to contribute to a deeper understanding of one's self in relation to a highly politicized world, left the high school students confused about purposes and their role in making self-determining choices within the context of the project. As Kincheloe and Steinberg point out, "problem detecting and the questioning that accompanies it become a form of world making in that the way these operations are conducted is contingent on the system of meaning" (305). Theater as a form of meaning making and interpretation of lived experience requires more time and orientation than the project first allowed.

Various current constructions of community service learning use language like the "doers and the done-to," "helpers and the helped," "agents and clients," "reformers and reformed."[5] These unilateral and nondimensional descriptors diminish the reciprocity and potential for mutual growth that could benefit both groups of students. Since the college course, like my high school class, is informed by various interpretations of Freirean critical theory, the outcomes for both groups of students have been institutionally defined by the roles they have assumed and been assigned as students enrolled in a credit course, either at the high school or at the university. In some measure these student roles conflicted and constrained the possibilities for participants since their work responded to course requirements.[6] Had all the students been reading Freire and Boal while openly discussing the theory underlying the project, their goals could have been more mutually constructed.

The Social Life of the Group

The social life of this group was defined by particular kinds of interactions. As mentioned above, questioning played a central role in defining how individual students interacted within the group. Asking questions not only served a gatekeeping function throughout the course of the project by redirecting the high school students toward a construction of theater congruent with the project's intention, but the questions also determined roles that the college students rejected but enacted nevertheless (Erickson and Schultz 151). The types of questions asked largely determined the social and political roles the questioner served in the life of the group. My analysis displays the ways in which questions were used to control conversational turn taking, to divert issues of control, and in some measure, to reveal the contradictions in Freirean critical theory as the students struggled to meet one another's needs as members of a group. The college students experienced even more difficulty in abandoning the rules of classroom discourse by denying their teacherly roles.

Critical theory challenges practitioners to "find forms within which a single discourse does not become the locus of certainty and certification" (Giroux 201). The theory supporting the collaboration simultaneously disrupted its process when critical theory's discourse imposed beliefs on the college students which they were not experienced enough to share or challenge. Victor, for example, saw the relevance of his choice to his life and wanted to examine it more globally. The college students interpreted this as a step away from his own experience without realizing just how close it really was. Rather than questioning their resistance to his choice, the college students questioned Victor's choice.

Kincheloe and McLaren identify "the hybridity endemic to contemporary criticalist analysis" (140). Given my questions about the portability of a critical theory project in a particular school setting, Freirean critical theory is itself being interrogated. From inside the high school, critical theory must be "ground(ed) contextually," in the words of Kincheloe and Pinar (20). The larger institutional forces that shape the local school culture—social, economic, linguistic, and political—form the project's backdrop. Words like "oppressor" and "oppressed" make collaboration impossible because they disempower the "other" group. This mutual "othering" or objectifying of the other reduces one's ability to act. In order to enact a liberatory pedagogy, some shared assumptions about goals and mutually constructed goals are necessary. Nancy Fraser's work in postmodern feminism supports this view. Fraser's postmodern critical theory helps us see the "overlapping alliances" and "vocabularies of contestation" which were generated by the students' discourse in their collaboration. By looking at critical theory (Freire's in particular as interpreted by Boal in *Theater of the Oppressed)* as it was applied in a local and particular context, I am responding to calls by Gore (1990), Ellsworth (1989), and Lather (1991) for more reflexive applications of a critical theory more broadly constructed. A useful enactment of critical theory will view collaborating partners as "agents involved in interpreting their needs and shaping their life-conditions rather than as potential recipients of predefined services" (Fraser 174).

Critical theory from inside the high school generated a dialectical relationship with the project which was designed outside the high school. The difference between critical theory as theory and critical theory as praxis emerged through looking at the way theory framed the college students' ideological orientation and understanding of their responsibilities to their high school counterparts and the requirements of their course. The roles they shared as students were complicated by the disproportionate responsibility the college group took upon itself for shaping the final outcomes of the project without sharing the reading, rationale, or open dialogue about the ideology behind the project. They also had a disproportionate investment in the outcome of the project, because the academic stakes were higher for the more privileged group, while the life stakes may have been greater for the high school students. At various points in the project, particularly at the beginning, the street theater politics disrupted the high school students' understanding of theater as imaginative play. While this was intentional, it ignored what the high school students brought to the project. Their understandings of theater, while conventional, were useful to their own enactment of identities which moved them beyond what students like Victor and Diego demonstrated were significant enactments of new "possible selves." At the same time, such an emphasis left the college students in the position of advocating for and coercing the high school students into a type of performance which conflicted with their preference and their understanding of theater and theatrical performance.

The confusion over and struggle with terminology is one of the difficulties expressed by the college students in their journals. I share a concern with Michael Apple that there exists a "danger of our own kind of mystification" (177). Victor, Diego, and Eve expressed their needs as students, often in ways that conflicted with the goals set and articulated by the college students. Nevertheless, the completion of the project depended in part on their knowledge and ability to act on that knowledge.

Choice, Chance, and Change

For months I wrestled with my conflicted writing about the struggle the college students had in negotiating the terms of their course objectives with the needs of the high school students. In a conference paper, I repeated this story, including my own partiality, by putting a negative spin on the lopsided collaboration which was consistent with a literature review on collaborations between urban schools and more powerful institutions. But the causes of collaborative failure and remedies for improving collaboration were not identified.

Likewise, my initial response to the project focused on the college students' difficulty in working under the political and ideological frame of Freirean critical theory. I too had failed to account more precisely for the problems. The part that questions played in obstructing their understandings of their roles emerged in my rethinking the effects of their difficulty in working within a theoretical frame imposed on their social relations with the high school students. Subsequently, their interactions were negotiated around the liberatory discourse of critical theory. On the other hand, the high school students' participation, investment, and agency in the theater project was measured by their willing interactions with the college students, a much less complicated assessment.

Since my initial attempt at writing about the project was filled with contradictions and biased assumptions, it seemed valuable to rehearse that turnaround in the interest of articulating what Gloria Anzaldúa calls the "in-between" worlds of academic and work cultures in which theories have the power to silence as well as empower. My roles as teacher, graduate student, and project collaborator not only gave me multiple perspectives on the project but complicated my reading of it as well. Since the project continues to grow and mature with each semester, what we as a group are learning about how language helps open us to possibilities, contributes further to our understanding of how best to encourage more openings within the project.

Implications

What difference did this project make in the lives of the students involved, the school in which it was set, or to the teachers who planned and revised it? While I've spent time over the past five semesters reviewing its goals and strengths, its shortcomings and failures, I've learned in the course of the project that collaboration requires constant rebuilding and ongoing revision if it is to fulfill goals of social change.[7]

The project informs other school/university collaborations by demonstrating the need to modify initial goals in order to align insider and outsider conventions. The implications of this work impact educational research in a number of ways. First, it raises questions about the use of critical theory and "empowering" pedagogies. Related studies on critical-theory-based writing pedagogies already exist, and to some extent inform this study.[8]

In turn this study informs sponsors of projects by offering an insider's perspective on a school-based collaboration. From inside schools, empowering pedagogies depend as much on the agency of those we seek to empower, particularly when they may or may not share beliefs or values with sponsoring partners. Carole Edelsky points out how "all projects are necessarily partial and contingent" (7). To take advantage of the existing potential within projects, it is essential to rethink the practices within them and to challenge even partially hegemonic practices.

Freirean critical theory itself became the object of interrogation as the analysis of student discourse probed the social organization of the project, discovered the friendships which developed between some of the students, and precipitated shifts in relations of power throughout the project. The discursive practices of both groups of students revealed ways in which they experienced the project differently as they learned about themselves as well as about one another. The high school students took advantage of opportunities throughout the project to try on various identities and imagine new ways of being. From a teacher's perspective, this reinventing of life stories created a sense of possibility the high school students expressed through the roles they chose for their performances, illustrating what Giroux calls "emancipation of the imagination." The high school students' discourse made the importance of imaginative play evident throughout the project.

And finally, why is it that this group of night school students continued coming to school, determined to make it? In spite of a 50 percent dropout rate, what kept the other 50 percent actively pursuing an education? What did they see in that education that the others didn't? Why aren't we hearing more of their stories? When we read about successes in urban districts, it is often in the form of institutional innovation—Central Park East, for example. But we know that there are thousands of young people who succeed in the thousands of other urban schools as well, in spite of the institutional failures loading the odds against their success. What compels them to persist in systems that are not consistently serving them well? Why don't we know more about them?

In a word, this story is a rebuttal to the *Last Chance* syndrome that constructs school and schooling as the last frontiers of hope for urban youth whose intelligence, resilience, and willfulness often defy the odds against them, yet find too little representation in the literature. I am not denying the harsh realities of many students' lives and the often difficult conditions of their schooling. I am, however, attempting to hear their stories of school as told by them from the inside in spite of these conditions. I hope it is a re/vision of school as a place students see as meaningful and useful to their needs as they take their places in the world.

We read one story after another accounting for failure in urban schools: Why there "Ain't No Makin' It," how dropouts are framed, why blacks are resistant in high school, the "Savage Inequalities" of the conditions of schooling, and how minority youth are silenced and oppressed. With few affirmations in the stories coming out of urban schools, there is little surprise that those of us working in these schools feel harassed by research, as often as not, and have to struggle to maintain dispositions which reject the totalizing failure so often described, documented, and displayed in research. At what point does the bad news become a self-fulfilling prophecy of hopelessness and despair? As a researcher consumed by the passionate voices of desperation in the literature, and as a classroom teacher equally passionate in her concern and commitment to those who return to the classroom day in and day out with an expectation that being there makes sense, I wanted to tell a different story from inside one urban classroom. It is not a simple story. If failure is as complex as research documents, success under the circumstances that these students achieved it is equally complex and equally important to study and document.

Notes

1. Henry Ford High School is a comprehensive public school with grades nine to twelve. At the time of the project the school offered two alternative programs to accommodate students in addition to day school, Extended Day School and Night School. In 1996 Governor Engler and the Michigan legislature cut funding for adult education, thus eliminating these alternative programs.

2. For a comprehensive discussion of students in alternative school settings, see Stevenson and Ellsworth (1993).

3. LeCompte (1995) writes about community organizers in the critical tradition who take into account their own power, agenda, and voice when entering

collaboration. Her work in Chicago Public Schools illustrates the complexity of collaboration.

4. Sinclair and Coulthard (1975) introduce the discourse of questions in class-rooms focusing on teacher/student interaction. Later studies by Cazden and Hymes (1982), Cazden (1988), Gumperz (1986), Goffman (1963; 1981), Tannen (1988), Gee (1990), and Schiffrin (1994) further explore the use of questions in classroom interactions between teachers and students.

5. Separate and distinct bodies of literature have developed around collabo-ration and service learning. Although they may intersect or overlap at various points, their motives, affiliations, and outcomes are different. See Radest (1993) for a broad discussion of service learning and community service. Gartner and Reissman (1993) address problems surrounding "help" as a concept in interven-tion programs. Karasik (1993) focuses on the traditions within existing commu-nities for successful organizing rather than on white middle-class volunteerism. The theater project was not viewed as a service learning course by the instruc-tor Buzz Alexander or by me, but the language used by the college students in their journals and final papers indicated that *they* constructed themselves in the discourse of service learners.

6. Both groups of students were enrolled in classes for credit. While criteria for grading students was determined separately, the primary expectation was that students would attend all sessions, and participate fully in the weekly workshop and final performance.

7. I have not come to new understandings of the project's conflicting inter-ests alone. Through conversations with both high school and university students in the project, parents of project participants, school and district administrators, and with my collaborator, Buzz Alexander, I have gained a much broader per-spective on the outcome of the project. The implications for research which addresses ongoing and replicable projects depend on examinations of theories which ground both projects as well as theories developing out of their process.

8. For example, see Lensmire (1994).

Works Cited

Anzaldúa, Gloria, ed. 1990. *Making Face, Making Soul: Haciendo Caras.* San Francisco: Aunt Lute Foundation.

Apple, Michael. 1993. *Official Knowledge: Democratic Education in a Conserv-ative Age.* New York: Routledge.

Belenky, Mary Field, et al. 1986. *Women's Ways of Knowing: The Development of Self, Voice, and Mind.* New York: Basic.

Boal, Augusto. 1979. *Theatre of the Oppressed.* Tr. Adrian Jackson. London: Pluto Press.

Bourdieu, Pierre. 1992. *An Invitation to Reflexive Sociology.* Pierre Bourdieu and Loic J. D. Wacquant. Chicago: University of Chicago Press.

———. 1977. *Outline of a Theory of Practice.* Trans. Richard Nice. Cambridge: Cambridge University Press.

Bourdieu, Pierre, and J. Passeron. 1977. *Reproduction: In Education, Society and Culture.* London: Sage.

Burbules, Nicholas C. 1993. *Dialogue in Teaching: Theory and Practice.* New York: Teachers College Press.

Cazden, Courtney. 1988. *Classroom Discourse: The Language of Teaching and Learning.* Portsmouth, NH: Heinemann.

Cazden, Courtney, Vera P. John, and Dell Hymes, eds. 1972. *Functions of Language in the Classroom.* New York: Teachers College Press.

Edelsky, Carole. 1991. *With Literacy and Justice for All: Rethinking the Social in Language and Education.* London: The Falmer Press.

Ellsworth, Elizabeth. 1989. "Why Doesn't This Feel Empowering? Working through the Repressive Myths of Critical Pedagogy." *Harvard Educational Review* 59: 297–324.

Erickson, F., and J. Schultz. 1981. "When Is a Context: Some Issues and Methods in the Analysis of Social Competence." Eds. J. Green and C. Wallat. *Ethnography and Language in Educational Settings.* Norwood, NJ: Ablex. 147–60.

Foucault, Michel. 1980. *Power/Knowledge: Selected Interviews and Other Writings, 1972–1977.* Ed. C. Gordon. New York: Pantheon Books.

Fraser, Nancy. 1989. *Unruly Practices: Power, Discourse and Gender in Contemporary Social Theory.* Minneapolis, MN: University of Minnesota Press.

Freire, Paulo. 1981. *Pedagogy of the Oppressed.* Trans. Myra Bergman Ramos. New York: Continuum.

Gartner, A., and F. Reissman. 1993. "Pitfalls of Help: Making Sure Helping Helps." *Social Policy* 1: 36.

Gee, James P. 1996. *Social Linguistics and Literacies: Ideology in Discourses.* London: Taylor and Francis.

Giroux, Henry A. 1988. *Schooling and the Struggle for Public Life: Critical Pedagogy in the Modern Age.* Minneapolis: University of Minnesota Press.

Goffman, Erving. 1963. *Stigma: Notes on the Management of Spoiled Identity.* Englewood Cliffs, NJ: Prentice-Hall.

———. 1981. *Forms of Talk.* Philadelphia: University of Pennsylvania Press.

Gore, Jennifer. 1990. "What Can We Do for You! What Can We Do for You? Struggling Over Empowerment in Critical and Feminist Pedagogy." *Educational Foundations:* 5–26.

Gumperz, John. 1986. *Discourse Strategies.* New York: Cambridge University Press.

Heidegger, Martin. 1966. *Discourse on Thinking.* Trans. John M. Anderson and E. Hans Freund. New York: Harper and Row.

Karasik, Judy. 1993. "Not Only Delicious Bowls of Soup: Youth Service Today." *Visions of Service: The Future of the National and Community Service Act.*

Washington, D.C.: National Women's Law Center and American Youth Policy Forum.

Kincheloe, Joe L., and Peter McLaren. 1994. "Rethinking Critical Theory and Qualitative Research." Eds. N. Denzin and Y. Lincoln. *Handbook of Qualitative Research*. London: Sage.

Kincheloe, Joe L., and William Pinar. 1991. *Curriculum as Social Psychoanalysis: The Significance of Place*. Albany: SUNY Press.

Kincheloe, Joe L., and Shirley Steinberg. 1993. "A Tentative Description of Postformal Thinking: The Critical Confrontation with Cognitive Theory." *Harvard Educational Review* 63: 296–320.

Lather, Patricia. 1991. "Staying Dumb? Student Resistance to Liberatory Curriculum." In Lather, Patricia, *Getting Smart: Feminist Research and Pedagogy With/in the Postmodern*. New York: Routledge. 123–52.

———. 1991. *Getting Smart: Feminist Research and Pedagogy With/in the Postmodern*. New York: Routledge.

LeCompte, Margaret D. 1995. "Some Notes on Power, Agenda, and Voice: A Researcher's Personal Evolution toward Critical Collaborative Research." Eds. Peter L. McLaren and James M. Giarelli. *Critical Theory and Educational Research*. Albany, NY: SUNY Press. 91–112.

Lensmire, Timothy. 1994. *When Children Write: Critical Re-visions of the Writing Workshop*. New York: Teachers College Press.

Markus, H., and P. Nurius. 1986. "Possible Selves." *American Psychologist,* 41: 954–69.

Radest, H. B. 1993. *Community Service: Encounter with Strangers*. Westport, CT: Praeger.

Schiffrin, Deborah. 1994. *Approaches to Discourse*. Cambridge: Blackwell Publishers.

Schutzman, Mady. 1994. "Brechtian Shamanism: The Political Therapy of Augusto Boal." Eds. M. Schutzman and J. Cohen-Cruz. *Playing Boal: Theatre, Therapy, Activism*. London: Routledge. 137–56.

Sinclair, J. M., and R. M. Coulthard. 1975. *Towards an Analysis of Discourse: The English Used by Teachers and Pupils*. London: Oxford University Press.

Stevenson, R. B., and J. Ellsworth. 1993. "Dropouts and the Silencing of Critical Voices." Eds. L. Weis and M. Fine. *Beyond Silenced Voices: Class, Race, and Gender in United States Schools*. Albany, NY: SUNY Press. 259–71.

Tannen, Deborah, ed. 1988. *Linguistics in Context: Connecting Observation and Understanding*. Norwood, NJ: Ablex.

Usher, Robin, and R. Edwards. 1994. *Postmodernism and Education*. London: Routledge.

Weis, Lois, and Michelle Fine, eds. 1993. *Beyond Silenced Voices: Class, Race, and Gender in United States Schools*. Albany, NY: SUNY Press.

12 Implementing Speaking and Listening Standards: Information for English Teachers

Nancy Rost Goulden

Without a great deal of warning or preparation, many English teachers find themselves in the position of being responsible for an expanded English curriculum that includes not only the traditional language arts of writing and reading but also the "new" language arts of speaking, listening, and media literacy. This paradigm shift that overtly includes and elevates the position of oral language arts in the English classroom is largely the result of the standards movement at both the national and state levels (Brewbaker 81).

The National Council of Teachers of English and International Reading Association's *Standards for the English Language Arts* explicitly names "listening, speaking, viewing, and visually representing" in the overall goal statement and includes terms that refer to the oral language arts in nine of the twelve standards (103). A study that examined twenty-nine state standards documents revealed that every program included both speaking and listening as part of the state standards (Goulden 200).

With such a strong imperative, it is clear that, throughout the nation, English teachers will be making changes in what they teach. Those who have not been formally trained in speech education will need assistance in revising local curriculum and in preparing to implement speaking and listening instruction in their classrooms. Initial efforts to bridge knowledge and background gaps will of necessity take place at the local or personal level through inservice training for and self-education by teachers already in the English classroom.

Reprinted from *English Journal*, September 1998.

Teachers charged with increasing the scope of speaking and listening instruction in their classrooms need help in two areas: (1) general information about what the content areas of "speaking" and "listening" include and how in a practical way teachers can incorporate appropriate instruction for these two language arts, and (2) specific information about the *processes* of speaking and listening that teachers can use when planning instruction, assignments, and assessments.

General Understanding of Speaking and Listening

What Do Speaking and Listening Mean?

Without a professional definition to guide them, teachers may erroneously assume that any vocalizing is speaking and any silent, passive behavior is listening. The Speech Communication Association's standards document clarifies the boundaries of what "speaking" and "listening" include as the terms are used by the speech communication discipline.

Based on the SCA guidelines, "speaking" includes both spontaneous informal speech (e.g., talking in work groups, responding in class discussion, participating in interviews) and prepared formal speeches. Speaking instruction focuses on expected behaviors (responses, delivery) in both formal and informal settings and the process of composing speech text (Speech Communication Association). Although they are worthwhile classroom activities, oral reading, acting, and reciting are not technically "speaking," and teachers should not assume that a curriculum limited to these oral activities fulfills speaking standards.

The SCA's explanation of "listening" is centered on a person's engagement in a complex active process. Curriculum revisions might focus on learning about the elements included in the listening process and also learning strategies for listening for a variety of purposes (SCA 1–2).

How Can Teachers Add Speaking and Listening to a Full Curriculum?

There is a way to give students instruction, practice, and feedback about their speaking, listening, and viewing without deleting significant portions of the curriculum that focus on reading, writing, and literature. The key is integrating the three newcomers into the base of the traditional language arts.

Many language arts programs have already incorporated informal speaking as an integral part of the curriculum through small group work in writing workshops and literature discussion. The vignettes in *Standards for the English Language Arts,* designed to illustrate standards in practice, provide model examples of the use of informal speaking and listening integrated into literature and writing study. Eleven of the twelve middle school and high school vignettes presented in the NCTE-IRA publication include either informal speaking in the contexts of group discussion, or interviews, or both. A few examples of individual speaking presentations are also found in the vignettes (55–67).

An excellent illustration of how to integrate individual speaking, discussion, and listening is found in Rodney Keller's approach to teaching writing called the "rhetorical cycle." He leads his students through the stages of the rhetorical cycle as they develop individual written compositions. His stages include: (1) background *reading* from literature or on a specific topic; (2) individual *thinking* stimulated by prewriting activities; (3) *speaking* in small groups about each writer's tentative plans; (4) *listening* and reflecting on the listener's understanding of their plans; and (5) *discussing* each student's proposal. Keller explains that, at the end of step 5, students have not only completed the prewriting phase, they have created an oral draft of their essay (27–32).

A second economical approach to integrating speaking and listening into the studies of reading and writing is to build on the commonalities between the pairs of language arts. Both teachers and their students need to talk about and identify the similarities and the differences that exist between reading and listening and between writing and speaking.

Just as a teacher might guide students to focus on the purpose (or genre) of a text students read in order to identify specific strategies for understanding, a teacher would also introduce the purpose for a listening episode to help students utilize the most appropriate listening strategies in that situation. Another potential commonality is the use of student responses to assess both reading comprehension and listening comprehension. Instruction that identifies a variety of appropriate listening response strategies (e.g., paraphrasing, questioning, extending) and then gives students practice with those strategies may overlap or at least correspond with reading instruction. A teacher can also adapt aids such as reading guides or graphic organizers to help students make meaning when listening. The Michigan State Board of Education's language arts standards document provides a good model for correlating the teaching of reading, listening, and viewing (4).

Both writing and speaking are fundamentally discourse composition processes. At the most general level, the processes encompass analogous stages: pre-composition (prewriting); oral drafting (written drafting); revision; speaking (writing); postspeaking (postwriting). However, the two processes in detail are not identical because of the different nature of the products and the different delivery systems. Teachers and students need to recognize that one does not write a text using the language, strategies, and conventions of written discourse, then read the paper out loud and call it a speech. The distinct language, syntax, and conventions of speaking, such as obvious sharing of the structure of the speech and repetition, are needed because of the transitory nature of the speech.

Building on the unique nature of each of the language arts and how they complement and intersect with each other is not only an efficient way to include speaking and listening, but also offers additional opportunities for practicing the common elements and processes that reading and writing share with listening and speaking.

Specific Instruction in Speaking and Listening

Speaking

The appropriate place to begin working with students on developing their speaking abilities is in the context of informal speaking. Extensive practice in exploratory talk and brief impromptu messages to the whole class create the foundation for students' preparation and presentation of longer more formal individual speeches.

Informal Speaking

Very little direct instruction is needed for informal speaking. The teacher's primary responsibility is to create classroom situations that promote active participation by all students in productive classroom talk. Most informal classroom talk will be either in the whole class setting, with students speaking to the entire class from their seats, or in small groups. There are three steps to encourage informal speaking participation by all students: (1) both teacher and students should expect every student to speak orally every day about class content; (2) the teacher should set up classroom structures and practices that make universal classroom speaking a reality; and (3) students should be given information and tools to prepare them to speak.

Perhaps the first rule of a fully participatory classroom is that the teacher will not depend exclusively on volunteers in class discussion. Students will learn that sometimes those who wave their hands will speak, but sometimes those who are sitting quietly will be asked to give a response. The purpose of calling on nonvolunteers is not to penalize the inattentive or reticent, but to set up the pattern of full participation.

To further develop participation expectations, teachers may use a technique called "go-rounds." This approach is first cousin to old-fashioned recitation. The teacher asks everyone to prepare a brief response to a question or prompt. This must be a response that all students are capable of producing. For example, if a piece of literature reveals a moral dilemma, each student might be asked to think of a moral dilemma they have experienced or observed. The teacher then goes around the room, directing students one-by-one to identify their moral dilemmas in no more than two sentences.

There is no need to collect all answers for every prompt. After several students have spoken, the teacher can move on to a second prompt and pick up the go-round using additional prompts until everyone in the class has had an opportunity to speak. If a particular student does not have a response, then that student is skipped for the time being but at the end of the sequence is asked again to respond.

Students need guidance in preparing to speak informally, either in small groups or before the whole class. Most people require a little thinking time before they orally explain, argue, or support an idea. Before turning students loose to "discuss this in your groups" or respond to a question requiring higher level thinking in class discussion, teachers should give students a few minutes to think about the topic and write some brief notes to explore and organize their thoughts. A good pattern for impromptu speakers to use is claim support. Students jot down a phrase or sentence that summarizes their answer and then map out the support for this central response claim.

The idea of everyone being an active contributor in class every day may be a new concept to students who have primarily experienced classrooms dominated by teacher talk or classrooms where the most assertive volunteers have participated in the classroom exchanges while other students played a passive role. Initially, the formerly silent students may be surprised and unprepared when asked to speak; however, when students realize that they are going to talk about class content, that they will have the opportunity to prepare to speak, and that their responses will be valued, then they are well on their way to being active participants in informal speaking. By making these recommended changes, the total amount of speaking time in the classroom does not have to change. The important change is the shifting pattern from minority participation to universal participation.

Formal Speaking

Once students have become reasonably comfortable with hearing their own voices and ideas in classroom discussion or recitation, they should be ready to move on to preparing and presenting short, simple individual speeches such as one-point speeches or narratives.

Teachers must lead students through the process of speech construction. As mentioned earlier, the foundations for the stage of precomposition should already be in place from their study of the writing process. However, the drafting stages for speaking and writing have important differences. In order to produce the appropriate word choices and sentence structure for the listening audience as opposed to the reading audience, the easiest method to ensure authentic oral language is by oral drafting and presenting the speech in an extemporaneous manner.

When using the extemporaneous mode, the speaker relies on detailed plans, extensive practice, and notes but does not create a written script. After speakers have researched the topic and chosen a thesis, audience outcome goals, main points, an organizational pattern, and support materials, they then make a detailed plan in the form of an outline, list, map, or any other note system that is preferred. The next step is to talk through the speech in a private setting following the written guide, stopping and restarting as needed, exploring alternative ways of expressing the message. By the time the speaker has worked through the speech, a rough oral draft exists. The next stage, of course, is revision based on a reevaluation of original choices. Speakers continue to individually and privately talk through the speech, perhaps several times, revising where needed.

When the speaker believes the speech is pretty well set, it should be timed and speaking notes prepared. In later run-through, speakers should become aware of delivery behaviors such as where they will stand, their posture, and vocal volume. Speakers may also want to get feedback from peers at this point and incorporate those suggestions before the final presentation.

The final text of the speech does not exist until the speaker presents the speech before an audience. In order to keep a speech fresh and spontaneous, the speaker should try to use slightly different language in each oral drafting session. These variations in language help build a backlog of different ways to express the same idea. Speakers then have a reservoir of word choices during the actual presentation if they have difficulty remembering or finding "the words."

Initially, students often find the idea of speaking without a written text frightening. In the oral communication field, we have found that teaching students the process of oral drafting and giving them sufficient practice, beginning with short simple speeches, helps them develop the confidence to speak in this natural, audience-centered manner.

The most important criteria by which to judge effective delivery is whether or not the speaker has made direct connection with the audience. Delivery that just looks or sounds polished will have little real impact if the speaker and audience are not engaged in shared communication. The real secret to effective delivery is attitudinal rather than behavioral. Successful speakers who appear natural and comfortable focus on the message and getting that message to the audience, not on how they look and feel. When a speaker is drawn into the excitement of the message, then effective delivery behaviors usually just happen.

Although experts do not recommend teaching a lengthy list of "do's" and "don't's" of delivery behaviors, some students may need specific feedback so they can reduce voice and body problems that interfere with audience connections. Typical feedback topics include reminders to speak loudly and clearly enough that the audience can hear the message without undue effort and to make genuine eye contact with audience members. Real eye contact requires that the speaker scan the audience and briefly lock eyes with individuals. This should not be a mechanical head swiveling, or a fixing of the speaker's eyes on the space above audience member's heads, or brief flickers of the eyes up and down. Instead, the speaker should look directly into the eyes of audience members for a very brief time. Some beginning students find it very difficult to make direct eye contact because they feel shy or self-conscious. Nevertheless, they should try to do so, since it is through sharing glances with audience members that they encounter supportive audience responses that can help increase their level of comfort.

Feedback is also necessary when students behave in ways that are so obviously distracting that their actions create barriers between the speaker and audience. An occasional "um" or small nervous movement probably will not even be noticed by the audience. It's not necessary to point out these minor natural flaws to speakers, since they are often reduced or eliminated as speakers become more comfortable in front of a group. On the other hand, speakers whose behaviors truly get in the way of the message (talking far too loudly; engaging in constant, undirected motion; or using frequent disfluencies or filler words) should be made aware of these problems in a private conference. Speakers may be able to achieve some level of control over such distractions once they realize what they are doing; however, if teachers assess speech delivery, they should remember that changing lifelong communication patterns is difficult and may not be possible except for very brief periods.

Speaking in Small Groups

Speaking in small groups is a special informal situation. Students are usually under less teacher supervision and have more independent responsibilities. Probably one of the easiest ways to include productive speech by every student every day is to take advantage of the cooperative learning that is already part of many language arts classrooms. In this less-controlled situation, though, it is easy for students to avoid being active participants or to revert to nonproductive or negative communication practices.

An excellent source for teachers who want to improve the communication aspects of small group work is the book *Focus on Collaborative Learning* published by NCTE. In the first two essays Dana Herreman and Richard Whitworth present concrete information on what students in the English classroom need to learn about small group communication (5–20). The following suggestions are in harmony with Herreman's and Whitworth's recommendations and also reflect current thinking and practices in the speech communication field.

First, enhancing the prospect of student active participation depends on the teacher's plans and instructions for small group work. The smaller the number of students working together, the greater the likelihood that all will participate. For active sharing by all, groups of three to five members work best. A second teaching strategy for stimulating total member participation is to give different responsibilities to different students within the group. For example, make each student responsible for a particular piece or category of information; or assign different communication tasks (e.g., paraphrasing the assignment to the group, summarizing the group decision or plan, reporting back to the whole group) to different individuals within the group.

It is important to provide direct instruction about communication in small groups on the following subjects: (1) making and using agendas; (2) eliminating negative communication behaviors such as being rude, using personal attacks, monopolizing the conversation, dominating the decisions and process, and being stubborn beyond reason; and (3) promoting behaviors that move the discussion along, such as asking pertinent questions, summarizing, providing useful information, and helping others enter the conversation. Self-assessment, peer assessment, and teacher observation can all be used to track and reinforce progress in these group communication practices.

Listening

Teachers should expect and facilitate good listening practices in all classroom settings. People attend to others' speaking when they have a motivation to listen. Some educators recommend that instructions or explanations be given only once. If students know they will hear something several times, they may just tune out altogether. Students may also ignore what classmates say if the exchange appears to be between only one student and the teacher. They just remain "on hold" until the student is finished speaking and wait for the teacher to tell them the "real answer." To break these passive patterns, teachers should remind students to direct their comments to the whole class. Rather than depending exclusively on teacher evaluation or reiteration of what a student has said, the teacher can hand the conversational baton off to another student by asking what the listener thinks of the first student's response or if the listener wants to add something to what has been said.

Content instruction in listening may be structured around purposes such as listening to acquire information, listening to analyze or evaluate, listening to extend empathy, or listening for entertainment. Concentrating on a specific purpose provides the framework for teaching students how to take notes, how to extract and identify organizational patterns from oral messages, and how to identify and test the arguments and reasoning found in oral and visual messages.

The richest classroom setting for students to practice and demonstrate proficient listening is in the small group context where they have maximum opportunities to respond. Teachers can introduce and model such listening response techniques as paraphrasing, summarizing, question-asking, evaluating, and turn-taking so that students will have an understanding of a variety of listening responses. Awareness of and responsibility for a menu of responses promotes active listening and gives students new tools for processing incoming data during a group discussion. Self, peer, and teacher assessment of response strategies used during small group discussion provide a means to guide students in the improvement of listening practices.

Conclusion

Teachers need not be overwhelmed by the prospect of implementing speaking and listening into the language arts curriculum. This article is not meant to be a prescription for implementation that must be rigorously followed step by step. Rather, it can serve as a guide to adding the new language arts to the traditional foundation. Implementation doesn't have to occur all at once. Teachers just need to start, learn what works in their classrooms, learn what others are doing, learn more about the field of oral communication, and then continue to integrate additional "new language arts" instruction and assignments.

Note

The Speech Communication Association has recently changed its name to the National Communication Association. More information can be found on their web site: www.natcom.org/.

Works Cited

Brewbaker, James M. "On Tuesday Morning: The Case for Standards for the English Language Arts." *English Journal* 86.1 (1997): 76–82.

Goulden, Nancy Rost. "The Roles of National and State Standards in Implementing Speaking, Listening, and Media Literacy." *Communication Education* 47 (1998): 194–208.

Herreman, Dana. "None of Us Is as Smart as All of Us." *Focus on Collaborative Learning: Classroom Practices in Teaching English, 1988.* Jeff Golub, chair, and the NCTE Committee on Classroom Practices. Urbana, IL: NCTE, 1988. 5–11.

Keller, Rodney D. "The Rhetorical Cycle." *The Leaflet* (1985): 27–32.

Michigan State Board of Education. *English Language Arts: Model Content Standards for Curriculum and Benchmarks.* Lansing, MI: Michigan Department of Education, 1996.

National Council of Teachers of English and International Reading Association. *Standards for the English Language Arts.* Urbana, IL and Newark, DE, 1996.

Speech Communication Association. *Speaking, Listening, and Media Literacy Standards for K through 12 Education.* Annandale, VA: SCA, 1996.

Whitworth, Richard. "Collaborative Learning and Other Disasters." *Focus on Collaborative Learning: Classroom Practices in Teaching English, 1988.* Jeff Golub, chair, and the NCTE Committee on Classroom Practices. Urbana, IL: NCTE, 1988. 13–20.

This book was set in Optima and Trajan by
City Desktop Productions.
The typeface used on the cover was Trajan.
The book was printed by Versa Press.